furniture care:

REPAIRING & RESTORING tables

furniture care:

REPAIRING & RESTORING tables

professional techniques to bring your furniture back to life

WILLIAM COOK
W. J. COOK & SONS
PHOTOGRAPHY BY **JOHN FREEMAN**

LORENZ BOOKS

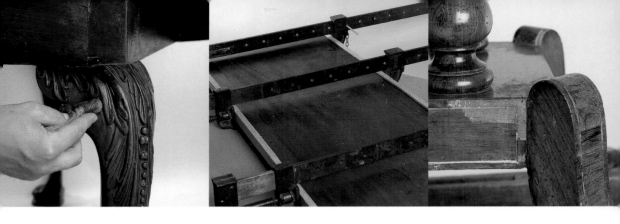

This edition is published by Lorenz Books
an imprint of Anness Publishing Ltd
108 Great Russell Street
London WC1B 3NA
info@anness.com

www.lorenzbooks.com; www.annesspublishing.com

If you like the images in this book and would like to investigate using them
for publishing, promotions or advertising, please visit our website
www.practicalpictures.com for more information.

© Anness Publishing Ltd 2014

A CIP catalogue record for this book is available from the British Library.

Publisher: Joanna Lorenz
Project Editors: Charlotte Berman, Lucy Doncaster and Claire Folkard
Text Editor: Alison Bolus
Designer: Lisa Tai
Photographer: John Freeman
Technical Director: Paul Lyon, W. J. Cook & Sons
Production Controller: Pirong Wang

Previously published as part of a larger volume,
The Complete Guide to Repairing and Restoring Furniture

PUBLISHER'S NOTE
Although the advice and information in this book are believed to be accurate and
true at the time of going to press, neither the authors nor the publisher can accept
any legal responsibility or liability for any errors or omissions that may have been
made nor for any inaccuracies nor for any loss, harm or injury that comes about
from following instructions or advice in this book. Before you begin any
restoration task, you should know how to use all your tools and equipment
safely, and be sure and confident about what you are doing.

CONTENTS

INTRODUCING TABLE RESTORATION

Whatever the date, period or style, every table eventually needs repair or restoration by its very nature. The approach has varied over the years. In the past, repairs were carried out by the original cabinet-maker or the local estate joiner. Until tables from earlier centuries became valued as antiques, repairs were often simply fashioned to make the piece usable, sometimes not even in the timber of the original. Today it is a different story.

Before the burgeoning interest in antiques, tables were considered as little more than secondhand pieces of furniture. It was not uncommon for tables that had worked loose to be strengthened by elaborate blacksmiths' brackets, which, ironically, took more time to make than knocking apart the table and repairing it correctly. But two major changes have taken place over time: the table has assumed its own character and it holds an ever-increasing value.

Understanding the construction of a table, including the cabinet-making techniques used during its period, is vital.

Just as important is access to the correct tools, a suitable work environment and, when necessary, antique timbers to patch damaged areas. Before beginning any restoration project all possible problems should be analysed and the best solutions realized. Otherwise, the easiest of tasks can soon develop into a major undertaking. It makes no sense to begin glueing a table together, only to discover that a cramping jig is needed. Equally, if a leg needs to be knocked apart from its gate and the dowel pegs, which are typical of table-making in the 17th and 18th centuries, have not been drilled out, then

the result will be a badly smashed mortise and tenon joint – leading to a much bigger job. Increasingly, research is needed to work out what was originally present but has subsequently been lost or changed – for instance, galleries, mounts or mouldings may have been altered or replaced to suit contemporary fashion. The aesthetics of a table can be rebalanced just by correctly replacing a later addition or by returning the table to its original height or proportion.

A huge responsibility rests upon the shoulders of the antique table restorer. In front of him is a piece of history, often

Above: *A selection of smith-made brackets, which were used as temporary strengtheners on loose furniture.*

Right: *A requirement of any serious workshop is an adequate breaker store. This will consist of timbers dating from the 17th, 18th and 19th centuries, hopefully to match the colour, grain and texture of pieces such as this George III card table, and to create a seamless repair.*

Right: *To retain the quality of this rosewood centre table, its colour and patination must be kept intact when restoring.*

with a surface that has developed its unique qualities over centuries. This uniqueness can be lost in an instant if the restorer applies the wrong methods. An understanding of colour and surface is vital because while previously the restorer would pass the table to the polisher to perform any necessary colouring, polishing or waxing, it is now common to find a restorer being both cabinet-maker and polisher. It is this skill of knowing how and what to do – and in many cases what not to do – that is the difference between a competent restorer and an amateur. So if in doubt, always consult an experienced restorer.

Those who can handle the tools of antique restoration correctly should consider further education. Restoration courses can range from a few months to one, two or three years. However, nothing will replace the hours spent at the bench, honing and developing one's skills and working alongside experienced restorers.

There is some debate concerning restoration versus conservation: whether with the use of old or breaker pieces of timber a table should be returned to a state in which the work is, as far as possible, unnoticeable, or whether repairs should be carried out sympathetically but

without blurring the line between old and new. While both sides have merit, from a commercial perspective seamless restoration wins the argument.

The importance of the restorer is increasing greatly as both the trade and public are buying more antique tables that require attention before they can be sold or used. The next generation inheriting tables are realizing the value and workmanship of their legacies. They know that their tables must be well cared for and restored if they are to survive.

Those who are prepared to learn their craft thoroughly while building up their historical knowledge, not to mention their supplies of timber, and increasing their practical ability, can be assured of a rewarding interest or career. As with everything in life, what one puts in is what one takes out – never more so than in the field of antique table restoration.

Below: *Today, the restorer acts as polisher too and must be able to polish entire table tops and not just colour in small repairs.*

HISTORY OF TABLES

The table has to be one of the most varied types of furniture in existence, with its role over the centuries being developed to suit numerous requirements ranging from business to functional to aesthetic. To trace the table's history one has to delve back to a much earlier period when furniture was scarce and great importance was placed on what little there was. While the earliest examples were basic in their design, they rapidly evolved.

During the medieval period, the dining table would be found in the great hall of the manor. There would usually be a dormant table at which the master and mistress plus any family members or favoured guests would sit. This table, often massive in size, would consist of a thick-planked top with a jointed underframe supported on large, bluster-turned legs, themselves joined by low stretchers. The room might also have further tables with planked tops, but these were of trestle construction and could be dismantled with the removal of pegs holding the supports in place to allow for dancing after the meal.

An interesting development during the 16th century was the draw table, where pull-out leaves were added to the basic refectory table design. Smaller tables that could be drawn up to the fireplace in winter, known as cricket tables, were also being used, and, like the refectory tables,

Left: *A late 17th-century oak gateleg table designed to seat eight people.*

were made from oak. They were basic in their construction, with a round top supported on three turned legs. With the exception of variations to the carved decoration, the basic model of the refectory or draw table remained fairly similar through to the 17th century.

During the latter part of the 17th century, dining in the great hall went out of fashion. New manor houses were being built with smaller, more intimate rooms, and these demanded a new style of table. The gate-leg table, designed to seat between eight and ten people, had a

Left: *The planked-top refectory dining table with its heavy carved base was popular from medieval times through to the 17th century.*

rectangular top similar to the refectory table but with two rounded flaps, which were hinged on one side and allowed the table to be folded down when not in use. Usually made from oak, but sometimes from walnut, these tables rapidly overtook the refectory, which was now made on a smaller scale and demoted to a buffet or side table. Other small tables were also produced to act as side or perhaps writing tables; their appearance owed much to the refectory table.

In European furniture, elaborate and gilded tables began to appear in the finest stately houses and palaces. Tables covered in gesso and carved detail were much prized, but it was not until the mid- to late 17th century that tables designed for a particular role began to develop their own distinctive style and character.

Cards were introduced to Europe during the 15th century, and gambling with dice was then also commonplace, but it was not until the late 17th century that specific tables for playing cards and gaming were made in any great numbers. The earliest card tables were usually veneered in walnut, with fold-over tops supported on single or double gates. Their evolution developed through the 18th century, with the only variations being the wood used and the type of embellishment

Left: *As gambling became an increasingly popular pastime from the late 17th century onward, elaborate gaming or card tables were made by the cabinet-makers of the period.*

added. Early tops were lined in velvet or needlework, but by the early 18th century baize was more popular. The main stylistic change came during the 19th century, when the gate-leg frame was replaced by four separate legs or a central column standing on a platform base on which the top would revolve before being supported on the carcass frame.

The introduction of the use of mahogany in furniture making during the early 18th century prompted another stylistic change. Underframes became much lighter, stretchers were removed

and legs, following the trend of the time, became more cabriole in profile, with carved lion paw or pad feet. With the increasing size of the country house and the fashion for entertaining on a larger scale, longer tables were now made. At first these were supported by numerous legs, but this soon gave way to the pedestal table, which was more elegant and user-friendly. These tables, sometimes able to seat 20 people, developed in the same form through the 18th and 19th centuries, with only the style and form of the bases changing to match the fashions.

Left: *With the increased fashion for entertaining on a large scale, three-, four-, or five-pillar dining tables were commissioned for the large country houses of the 18th century.*

At the same time, another style of rectangular table evolved. This was designed to suit the fashion for smaller town houses and could be reduced in length to accommodate a varying number of diners. Various techniques were used to support the table tops, with concertina and pull-out bearers being incorporated. By the mid-19th century, however, numerous legs had been replaced by only four, and the weight of the table tops was supported by a central threaded metal draw bar operated with a winch-like handle inserted into the end.

As well as the larger dining table there was, of course, a need for smaller tables, known as breakfast tables. Originally designed so that the family could enjoy an intimate breakfast together rather than feel lost around a large pillar table, they quickly developed, especially during the latter part of the 18th century, to suit the growing number of smaller town houses.

Above: *A superb example of an 18th-century kettle stand.*

One interesting table is the Irish wake table. Made during the mid-18th century, this was a long oval with a narrow central section on to which twin hinged flaps were attached. During a wake, the coffin would be laid in the centre of the table, with the food and drink for the mourners placed on the raised flaps on either side.

A blossoming of interest in the arts, business and entertaining promoted the evolution of a whole range of tables from the 18th century onward. A ceremony that probably inspired more furniture-makers than most was the taking of tea, which became the social highlight of the day during the 18th century and was seen as an opportunity to flaunt one's wealth and social position. A wide range of tables connected to the tea ceremony sprang up, including kettle stands, often richly carved, on which the silver kettle would stand; urn tables with delicate legs on which the urn would sit; and silver tables, with their open-fret galleries, pierced brackets and elegant stretchers, which would sit central in the drawing room and on which the silver tea set would be placed. The tea table, similar to the card table but with a veneered interior rather than a baized one, would be ideal for sitting at, and small tripod tables with round tops would be placed beside the settees and chairs.

In the mid-18th century, small flap-tables began to appear; these had hinged brackets rather than gate-legs supporting the flaps. Known as Pembroke tables, they were used to breakfast on or as ladies' writing tables. Another new appearance was the drum table, with a circular top and number of built-in drawers, which furnished offices and libraries.

In the drawing room, large pier tables, evolved from the earlier card and side tables, were placed on either side of windows or fireplaces with the new fashionable pier glasses above them. Behind settees sat elegant sofa tables, which were longer, rectangular versions of the Pembroke table. In short, tables were designed and commissioned for almost

Above: *Although English in style, this outstanding 18th-century tripod is in fact American in origin. This illustrates how designs were carried across the Atlantic.*

every use in the 18th century. Their overall designs remained fairly unaltered throughout the 19th century, although more decorative inlays and woods were used, the main difference being the gravitation toward a more robust style.

During the early years of the 20th century, furniture-makers such as Charles Rennie Mackintosh (1868–1928) showed a wide virtuosity in table design, but it was not until the 1920s that function finally took precedence over form. Over the century, the emphasis on eating together faded, and the dining table became less central to the home. More meals were being eaten in the kitchen and the dining table was reserved for more formal occasions and entertaining. In its place sprang up coffee tables and, more recently, computer desks. Where once oak, mahogany or walnut were the only choice, now laminates, steel, chrome and plastic are all incorporated into the modern table.

TABLE CONSTRUCTION

Antique tables dating from medieval times to the early 20th century come in all manner of forms, each designed and made to undertake a particular role. The construction principles remain the same, however, although the joints used and degree of construction detail may vary. The earliest forms of refectory table, for example, consisted of little more than a planked top fixed to a trestle base, but over the years the aesthetics of the piece rapidly developed.

From the 15th century onward, table bases were held together with dowelled tenons, which were the strongest type of joint. When better adhesives appeared, the dowel in the joint was used less often.

When smaller gate-leg tables became fashionable, a new type of joint known as the knuckle joint was devised. This allowed part of the underframe, which was attached to the gate leg, to swing out, away from the main frame, and support the hinged part of the top.

When the sofa table first appeared later in the 18th century, it had twin end supports joined by a central stretcher. This stretcher gradually became lower as the bases became heavier. By the early 19th century the twin ends had often been replaced by a central column, which sat on smaller splay legs.

The legs of central column tables are fixed to the column with dovetailed tenons to ensure that the weight does not collapse the base. As an extra precaution, there will often be a metal strengthening bracket as well. With drum tables the column may pass through the underside of the top to allow it to revolve, and it is usually fixed with a birdcage movement – a removable wedge that allows the base and top to be disconnected.

Decoration became more important from the late 17th century onward. For instance, 18th-century open-fret galleries surrounding the tops of tea tables were there to prevent the service being knocked off. Their construction was one of the earliest forms of laminating, with three layers of veneer, each at right angles to the next layer to give added strength. The fret would be cut out from this laminate, and the gallery would be joined with small foxtail mitres, which involved using slithers of veneer as joining pieces.

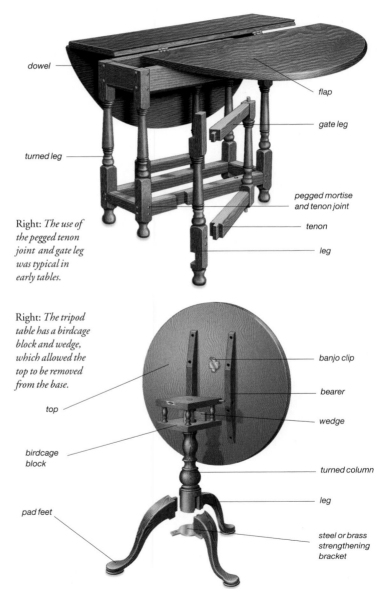

Right: The use of the pegged tenon joint and gate leg was typical in early tables.

dowel · flap · gate leg · turned leg · pegged mortise and tenon joint · tenon · leg

Right: The tripod table has a birdcage block and wedge, which allowed the top to be removed from the base.

top · birdcage block · pad feet · banjo clip · bearer · wedge · turned column · leg · steel or brass strengthening bracket

Tools, equipment and materials

The right tools, equipment and materials are the lifeblood of

any restorer. Often passed from generation to generation,

they must be cared for and used with the skill they deserve,

for without them even the most gifted of restorers will be

unable to undertake the most basic of restoration jobs.

CREATING A WORKSPACE

More often than not, financial limitations and space will dictate the location of a workshop. The most important piece of equipment in the workshop will be the bench, so it is important that any area under consideration should, as a basic requirement, be able to house both you and the bench, as well as allowing space for the furniture being restored. You will also need to surround yourself with tools and machinery, so plan your work area carefully.

YOUR WORKBENCH

Once you have decided where to site your workbench, you will need to assess the various factors that are vital for good work.

The most important factor is the quality of light available. Natural light is ideal, so, if possible, position the bench directly under a window or skylight. Hang fluorescent strip lights above the workbench and, if you are intending to undertake any polishing work, make sure that normal lights are also available (fluorescent light gives a false colour). Also paint the walls white to reflect, and so maximize, whatever light there is.

Rack your tools in an organized manner so that they are readily available. Keep groups of tools, such as hammers, saws or chisels, together for easy access. Keep tools that are not used daily, such as carving tools, carefully wrapped to protect their sharp edges, and stored neatly ready for use. Above all, keep the work area and bench clean and tidy.

Remember that most of your time will be spent standing at the workbench, so put blocks under it, if necessary, to set it at a height that is comfortable for you to work at. Also, if possible, opt for a wooden rather than a concrete floor, as concrete is very tiring on the feet and legs.

If space and funds permit, have two separate areas within the workshop: one for cabinet making and the other, in a dust-free area, for polishing. This dual use maximizes the available space.

An ideal workbench

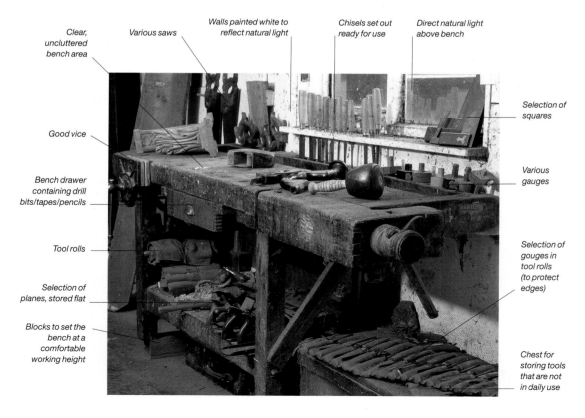

Clear, uncluttered bench area

Various saws

Walls painted white to reflect natural light

Chisels set out ready for use

Direct natural light above bench

Good vice

Selection of squares

Bench drawer containing drill bits/tapes/pencils

Various gauges

Tool rolls

Selection of gouges in tool rolls (to protect edges)

Selection of planes, stored flat

Blocks to set the bench at a comfortable working height

Chest for storing tools that are not in daily use

YOUR TOOLKIT

When restoring antique furniture, the best tools are, without doubt, those that were originally used in the 18th and 19th centuries. For a hobby restorer, modern tools are a suitable, and realistic, substitute, but anyone wishing to pursue a career in the field of furniture restoration should endeavour to build up as wide a collection of antique tools as possible. Such tools were made by craftsmen for craftsmen. The steel used then is still the best for holding a suitable cutting edge now, and the handles, made from box or rosewood, feel more comfortable to the hand than modern materials such as plastic. Often you will see numerous names stamped into the handle of an antique tool, indicating how it has passed through the hands of generations of craftsmen.

Old tools can be found in a number of places, ranging from specialized tool auctions or car boot sales, to local fêtes and classified advertisements in the local paper. If you are really lucky, you may have the opportunity to buy the tools and contents of the workshop of a retiring cabinet-maker. If this happens, beg or borrow the funds to buy the tools, since such events are rare indeed.

In the absence of antique tools, or while you are building up your collection, start your toolkit by buying modern equivalents, but be sure to buy the best quality that is available within your budget. Clamps are an exception to this rule, and modern sash, snap and G-clamps are fine. These are expensive pieces of equipment, so it is a good idea to buy a few whenever you can afford them.

Modern screwdrivers, saws and chisels can be purchased to begin with, and you can gradually replace them with older examples if you want. Some tools and equipment, such as spring clips, can be made in the workshop.

Most cabinet-makers take a lifetime to build up their collection of tools, and almost all craftsmen will prefer to work with only their own tools, which, once purchased, should last a lifetime.

If you become interested in restoring then you may become an avid collector of tools yourself. Certainly, if you decide to take up restoring as a job, then building up your stock of tools and materials can be seen as an investment in your own future. Remember always to respect your tools, keeping them clean and sharp, and wrapping them safely whenever they are not in use.

Safety

The safety rules of a workshop are essentially those of common sense. Always remember that the workshop is potentially a dangerous area, so make sure that children cannot get in. Always handle sharp tools with care and replace them in their rack after use. Keep a regularly tested fire extinguisher close to hand and lock any flammable materials away in a fireproof cabinet. Keep the work area clean and tidy and sweep up all shavings at the end of the day. Good ventilation is important, especially when using stripper or any other chemicals. Make sure any stains or other liquids are kept in jars and clearly labelled. Wear suitable safety clothing as the job dictates. Tie back long hair, remove any dangling jewellery and always wear a long apron to protect your clothes.

Above: *A fire extinguisher is essential. Install a powder-filled fire extinguisher at every exit door.*

Above: *When using power tools likely to create a lot of dust or sparks, it is a good idea to wear a protective helmet.*

Left: *Basic safety equipment should include a first-aid kit, goggles, ear defenders, a filter mask, gloves and a disposable mask.*

SAWS AND MEASURING DEVICES

It is important that saws are kept in good condition because a sharp edge is essential, particularly when doing detailed work. Although modern power saws can take much of the effort out of sawing, and certainly have their place in a workshop, hand-held saws, such as the tenon saw, are invaluable for small-scale work. Measuring devices, including dividers, callipers and gauges, are the key to successful cabinet work, so look after them carefully.

SAWS

The three most commonly used saws in day-to-day restoration are the full tenon saw, the half-tenon saw and the dovetail saw, all of which have varying numbers of teeth per centimetre (inch). The more teeth per centimetre (inch), the finer the cut will be. Some of the finest cutting teeth are those of the fret and coping saws, designed for detailed shape work.

The large panel saw, used for cutting larger boards, comes with two teeth settings: the cross cut, designed to cut across the grain, and the ripsaw, designed to cut along the length of the grain. With the introduction of modern band saws and circular saws, large panel saws are used less frequently, but all workshops should have at least one of each type.

Saws will almost certainly be used on a daily basis and should be used only for the specific task for which they were designed. Using a fine dovetail saw for general work, for example, will damage the teeth and make it unsuitable for the finer work of cutting dovetails.

The saw is a precision cutting tool and should always be kept sharp and in good condition. While it is possible to sharpen the saw yourself, it is far better to send it to a professional saw doctor to have the teeth set and sharpened.

Above: *An extensive range of reliable measuring tools is essential for the furniture restorer to carry out accurate work.*

When using a saw on a particularly difficult piece of wood, rub a little candle wax on the blade to help ease the cutting.

MEASURING DEVICES

"Measure twice, cut once" is an old cabinet-makers' saying, and it is as true today as it has always been. Accurate measuring is vital, since if the measuring is inaccurate then all the work that follows is wasted, at worst possibly leading to a ruined piece of valuable furniture, at best meaning you have to start all over again. Measuring tools include dividers, marking gauges, callipers, set (carpenter's) squares, sliding bevels and box rules, all of which are indispensable. Double-check every measurement and work from a face edge (the first edge cut and planed level, which is then used to take other measurements).

Left: *Three saws from a typical workshop, each with a different number of teeth per centimetre (inch). The more teeth a saw has, the finer the cut will be.*

HAMMERS AND SCREWDRIVERS

Hammers, ranging from pin hammers for light work to heavier hammers for knocking apart furniture, are an essential part of any restoration work, as are the various types of mallet, particularly the carver's dummy, which is a very useful tool. A wide range of screwdrivers should also be kept to hand. Look out for examples with long and short shanks, which are useful in different situations. Be sure to keep the leading edge of a screwdriver sharp.

HAMMERS

The restorer will have two or three different types in the workshop, including the light pin hammer, the general cabinet hammer, which will be used on a daily basis, and a heavier hammer used to knock apart carcasses and drive in large nails. Hammers should never be used to hit another tool, such as a chisel – that is exclusively the role of the mallet.

When the face of a hammer becomes dirty and worn, file it flat then rub it lightly with fine-grade sandpaper to remove the dirt and score the surface. This enables the hammer to grip the head of the nail. This process, which is known as "dressing", will probably need to be done at least two or three times a month.

MALLETS

These were designed to be used against the handle of a tool such as a chisel or gouge. They come in different weights and shapes, and the greater the weight of the head, the more force it will exert. A good example of this is the carver's dummy, whose heavy lignum vitae head

Above: *Two traditional mallets – it is useful to have a selection in your workshop.*

ensures that a simple wrist action gives a very strong blow. It also means that the carver need not look at the mallet as it swings down, since its rounded head will always strike the tool being used, thus allowing the carver to concentrate fully on the work in hand.

Larger mallets are for roughing off, while lighter ones are for delicate work. The square-headed mallet is for general cabinet work and knocking apart, where a large hammer might bruise the wood.

SCREWDRIVERS

It is best to equip yourself with as wide a range of screwdrivers as possible. It is well worth spending a little time at car boot sales or trawling through second-hand shops in order to build a collection of traditional tools at a lower price than new ones. Old screwdrivers tend to have a longer shank, which gives better leverage. They also have handles made from box-wood or beech, which are kinder to the hand than plastic. Small screwdrivers with short shanks can be very useful for removing screws in awkward locations.

When buying an old screwdriver, check that the leading edge is straight and even. If it is worn or uneven, you will have to grind it flush, because a screwdriver that does not fit snugly into a screw-head slot can break the screw. Remember that a screwdriver is designed for removing and putting in screws and should never be used as a lever, which could damage the edge and bend the shank.

Below: *A selection of old screwdrivers with shanks of varying lengths.*

Holding a hammer

1 *When using a hammer, the most common mistake is to hold it half way down the handle in the belief that this allows more control and accuracy. In fact, it has the opposite effect.*

2 *The correct way to hold the hammer is at the end of its handle, which gives much better balance and control. When using a hammer, make several medium blows rather than trying to drive the nail home first time.*

SMOOTHING TOOLS AND CLAMPS

There are many different types of planes and clamps used in restoration work, and modern tools are very similar to their traditional counterparts. Some planes are fitted with their own guide fences and others with changeable blades, while moulding planes have specially shaped bases and blades for detailed shaping work. Different clamps, like planes, are designed for particular tasks and it is advisable to build up as wide a selection as possible.

PLANES

The earliest planes were made with wood bodies, but during the 18th and 19th centuries the metal-bodied plane took over, although the moulding planes remained wooden.

There are various examples of planes, each suited to a particular role, including the utilitarian jack plane, the smoothing plane, and the smaller block-and-shoulder plane for more intricate work. There are also specialized planes, such as moulding planes, with their specially shaped bases and blades, which are designed to cut the waist, base and other mouldings found on carcass furniture. However, the modern router, with its wide range of shaped cutters, has largely taken over this role. Although the spokeshave does not look like a plane, it is classed as one because it works along the same principle.

The blade of any plane is designed to cut the wood cleanly without tearing the grain, and so it is important that it is always kept sharp. When the blade is sharp and the plane is used correctly, it should made a wonderful slicing sound as it cuts through the wood.

SCRAPERS

The cabinet scraper, which is basically a piece of metal with a burred edge, is designed to clean up surfaces and remove any plane marks prior to sanding.

The most frequently used scraper will be a rectangular one for shaped mouldings, but tailor-made scrapers are also useful. The most common example is the French curve, which is shaped like a kidney and should be able to scrape any concave area.

Scrapers should always be used sharp and should produce shavings, not dust. To sharpen a scraper, you should draw a hard piece of rounded metal, such as the shank of a screwdriver, across the edge. This produces a burr, which is needed to cut the wood.

SANDING EQUIPMENT

The earliest types of sandpaper were, in fact, made from sharkskin, known as shagreen. It was dried and used very much in the same way as sandpaper is today. This was followed by the use of ground glass or sand, which was stuck to paper, and it is from this that the terms "glasspaper" and "sandpaper" are derived.

Nowadays there are many abrasive papers available, including silicon carbide, aluminium oxide and garnet paper, but the term "sandpaper" is still commonly used to describe them all. These papers are available in a number of different grits, or grades, with the most commonly used grits in the workshop ranging from 80 (the coarsest) to 320 (the finest).

Sandpaper is rarely used on its own but is wrapped around sanding blocks of cork or wood. If a specific moulding has to be sanded, you will need to make a shaped piece of wood (overloe) that matches the profile of the moulding, so that it can be sanded without having its shape altered. Over the years, the restorer will build up a wide selection of tailor-made overloes.

When you start sandpapering a piece of work, begin with the coarsest grade and work up through the grades to the finest. Wetting the wood between each grade, and allowing it to dry before you start with the next grade, will give a smoother finish. Also, if you intend to apply a water stain, this inter-grade wetting process will make sure that the grain does not rise at the staining stage.

Above: *A selection of planes showing some of the variety of shapes and materials used in their construction.*

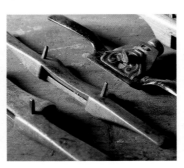

Above: *The spokeshave is a cross between a plane and a scraper, and is a very versatile tool for shaping wood.*

Above: *Overloes are specially shaped wooden blocks that are used with sandpaper to smooth the profile of a moulding.*

CLAMPS

These tools come in a wide variety of styles, each of which is suited to a particular role. The most common types are the long sash clamp, the G-clamp, which comes in different sizes, the band clamp, the snap clamp and the spring clip. Modern clamps are similar to traditional ones, and although they are fairly expensive to buy, it is best to have as wide a range as possible.

When working with clamps, always use clamping blocks to prevent bruising and the appearance of "hoof" marks on the wood. Also, never over-tighten a clamp: the pressure it exerts can cause structural damage to delicate pieces.

When gluing up a complex job, it is a good idea to have a "dry" run beforehand, working out which clamps will be used and in which order. Spending a little time doing this may prevent problems later on

when the glue has been applied and is setting. It also means that you will have everything you need to hand and will feel confident about starting the work.

Above: *A wide selection of modern and traditional clamps, including G-clamps and sash clamps, are essential for many types of restoration work.*

Making a band clamp

While most clamps can be bought, the steel band clamp is unique in that it is workshop made and tailored to a particular job in hand. Its role is to clamp an oval or round, creating an equal pressure around the circumference.

You will need a small block of hardwood, a steel band (as used for binding building materials), small screws and a clamp.

1 *Cut two lengths of the steel band to a length slightly shorter than the frame's circumference and punch two pilot holes into each end of them.*

2 *Using a metal bit, drill two small holes through the pilot holes. Be sure to place a scrap block of wood on the bench or worktop to protect it.*

3 *Use a countersink drill bit to countersink the two holes previously drilled. This will make sure that the screw heads are level with the band.*

4 *After marking the shape of the frame on the hardwood, use a band saw to cut the concave profile. Cut the block in half.*

5 *Screw the two lengths of steel band to the shaped side of the hardwood, making sure that the countersunk hole side of the band is used.*

6 *Finish by filing the screw heads flush with the metal band, this will make sure that no unnecessary scratching or marking occurs.*

7 *The band clamp in use. The hardwood blocks are clamped together to create the tension.*

CHISELS AND CARVING TOOLS

All these implements have their own jobs, which involve paring away wood in one form or another, but one rule applicable to all is to keep their edges sharp so that they can cut through wood and not tear the grain. If you are interested in carving, you will start to amass a large collection of tools, since each has its own specific function. In general, old examples tend to keep their edge longer than modern versions, due to the better-quality steel.

CHISELS

The cabinet-maker or restorer will have three main types of chisel to hand on the workbench. These are the paring chisel, the mortise chisel and the firmer chisel. Within these groupings there should be a range of widths suitable for any task.

The paring chisel, with its bevelled edges and long blade, is primarily used for paring, levelling and chamfering. It is designed for hand-use only and should never be struck with a mallet.

The mortise chisel, as its name suggests, is used to cut out mortises, and for this reason its blade is noticeably thicker than that of both the paring and firmer chisels. The thickness of the blade means that it can withstand a heavy blow from a mallet and a certain amount of leverage when removing the waste wood from a mortise.

The firmer chisel, with its shorter, thicker blade without a bevelled side, is designed for heavier work and can be used in conjunction with a suitable mallet.

CARVING TOOLS

The carver is one of the most skilled craftspeople in the field of antique restoration. The skill of carving is similar to that of a painter, except that the carver's medium is wood and the end results are three-dimensional.

The required tools, which can number into the thousands, are known individually for their suitabilities and strengths, and before undertaking a carving project the carver will select the required implements and sharpen them. Indeed, depending on the hardness of the wood, it is not unknown for a carver to resharpen a blade every few minutes during carving work.

Small carving tools are essential for detailed and intricate work. They provide much greater control of the task in hand, allowing the carver to remove small slivers of wood with the minimum of effort.

There are numerous types of carving tools, including scrolls, which set out the shape of the carving; V- or parting tools, which produce long sweeps; grounders,

Above: *While gradually building up a collection of antique tools, which you can find in second-hand shops, it is a good idea to purchase modern equivalents too.*

which remove the background waste; veiners, which carve the fine details, such as flowers, leaves, etc; and fish tails, which, like the grounders, help to remove unwanted wood.

While this procedure may seem very complicated, it is worth noting that the complexity and intricacy of much of the work means that it takes several years for a carver to reach full potential.

Each carving project can often take hundreds of hours of painstaking work, and, aside from patience, the main skill a potential carver needs to learn is the ability to be able to study an existing carving closely and to mimic exactly the hand in which it was originally carved. The real test of the master carver is to restore carving to the extent that the new work blends in seamlessly with the original detail.

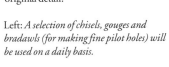

Left: *A selection of chisels, gouges and bradawls (for making fine pilot holes) will be used on a daily basis.*

Left: *A small selection of the many hundreds of carving tools required by the master carver.*

Above: *A carver's vice allows free and easy access to any carved piece held in it.*

Sharpening a chisel

Some of the tools most used by the cabinet-maker or furniture restorer are the various chisels. These are used to pare, level and shape the wood. It is vital that the chisels are kept sharp at all times, as failure to do so will result in them tearing the grain rather than slicing through the wood. When a chisel loses its edge, the process of re-honing takes only a few minutes, and the procedure is very simple.

1 *Using a grinding wheel and selecting the finest grade of the two stones, offer the chisel at an angle of approximately 25–30 degrees. Remove the bevel as soon as it is flat, otherwise the chisel's length will be shortened too much and its working life substantially reduced.*

2 *Lightly lubricate an oil stone with a fine oil, then draw the chisel repeatedly along the stone at an angle of 30–35 degrees. This will produce the cutting edge.*

3 *Turn the chisel over and lay it flat down on the stone. Rub it back and forth two or three times. This process, known as "backing off", will weaken the burr that has built up. Strop the chisel on a piece of leather, which should remove the burr.*

4 *Finally, use your newly sharpened chisel to cut a slither off a piece of wood. This will check for sharpness as well as removing the burr, should it not have come off on the leather strop.*

5 *The illustration shows how the finished edge should look if the chisel has been sharpened correctly.*

TURNING TOOLS

Since medieval times, turning has been used in the construction of furniture. While lathes have changed with the times – the earliest examples were human-powered – the basic techniques and principles used by the early bodgers (travelling lathe craftsmen) have remained much the same as they are today. Likewise, the tools used in modern workshops would still be recognizable to the turner of centuries past.

The tools of the turner are divided into measuring and turning tools. It is vital that accuracy is maintained, and this is done with the aid of the measuring tools: dividers to measure length and width and callipers to measure external or internal dimensions. Both take measurements from a template (pattern) and can be used easily when the lathe is in operation.

The turning tools, which have long blades and long handles to counteract the force of the lathe, are divided into four groups. First there are the gouges, which are used to rough off the wood to an approximate cylinder. Next are the skew chisels, used to refine the shape of the cylinder to its final form. The scrapers are used to make the grooves and turnings, and finally the parting tools are used to form long trenches and part the turnings from the waste wood.

Due to the stresses imposed on the tools they should be kept sharp and constantly checked for any possible stress fractures. This is one of the occasions when it is preferable for the restorer to use modern tools rather than their antique

equivalents. This is because the latter may have developed stress factors in their blades or faults in their handles, which, if fractured during application, could cause serious injury to the turner. It is also important, therefore, to make sure that the tools are always used correctly. Due to the potential risks involved when using a

Above: *A wide selection of measuring and turning tools is necessary to ensure that all turned work is accurate.*

lathe, it is essential to take an approved instructional course in turning before beginning lathe work (see Further Information, p.93).

Left: *The tap and die is a turning tool that is at the opposite end of the spectrum to high-speed lathes.*

Right: *Turning tools are distinctively different from woodworking chisels.*

Cutting a male screw thread

When turning and cutting a new thread, it is important to make sure that both male and female parts are of a corresponding size. As dies (internally threaded tools for cutting male threads) and screw taps (threaded steel cylinders for cutting female threads) exist in corresponding pairs, a match should be found. Remember that once you have started cutting, you must continue working until the thread is finished; stopping and starting will mean that you will not get a perfect match.

1 Select and cut a piece of wood that is slightly larger in width than the diameter of the thread that is being replaced.

2 Turn the wood with a large gouge. Measure the size of the die housing using callipers, then compare this measurement to the size of the turned wood.

3 Turn the column to the final diameter required, checking the measurements with the callipers as you work.

4 Place the turned column in the vice and, using a sharp chisel, cut a leading edge in the column. This will aid the beginning of the thread cutting.

5 Place the die, which has an inset cutting blade, on top of the turned column. Start turning it in a clockwise direction to cut the thread.

6 Keeping the die level, follow the technique of one full rotation clockwise followed by one half rotation counterclockwise. This clears the blade of shavings.

7 Continue all the way to the base and then remove the die. Remove the wood column and cut it to the required length.

Cutting a female screw thread

A corresponding female thread now needs to be cut to match the male thread. Should the female and male threads be of different sizes, a solution is to plug the female thread with a suitable piece of wood and then recut the female wood to a size to correspond with the male thread.

1 Place a piece of wood in a vice. Drill a corresponding hole into it of compatible size to the turned male thread, then pare a leading edge on the hole with a sharp chisel.

2 Grip the screw tap in the vice and place the leading edge on top of it. Turn the piece of wood one complete turn clockwise followed by a half turn counterclockwise.

3 When completed, the male and female parts should fit snugly together and the thread should work with ease.

MACHINERY

While antique restoration is traditionally a craft that relies on hand-held tools, the use of machinery can, in certain cases, make life much easier. It was the mass introduction of mechanized tools during the 19th century that radically altered furniture production. Although they can never replace the trained craftsman, the new generation of hand-held power tools available today will certainly save you many valuable hours in the workshop.

The use of heavy machinery in the restoration workshop is fairly limited. In fact, not many restoration workshops will have the space for a fully fitted machine shop, especially as the heavier types often require three-phase electricity supplies. (This involves installing a unit to boost the power from single to three phase, and is usually needed only in commercial workshops.) However, the inclusion of certain heavy machines can make life much easier, and two invaluable machines are the band saw and the lathe.

Hand-held machine tools, such as an electric or cordless drill, jigsaw and router, are a great help, and you should stock as wide a range of router cutters as possible. You could also buy a router bench, which extends the possibilities of the router. As finances and space allow, you can buy extra machinery, such as circular saws, thickness planers and pillar drills.

While these will not be used on a daily basis, they can save hours of effort when they are required. As with all machinery, it is vital that you obtain the correct training before using it (see Further Information, p.93) and that you always carefully follow the safety instructions.

BAND SAW

The band saw's blade is a flexible length of steel that runs in a continuous loop. It is ideal for cutting curves and angles or for trimming strips from wider pieces. Its limitations are governed by the depth of the sawbed and the thickness of the blade. Never apply undue pressure to the blade, as this will damage either it or the guiding rollers and cause the blade to snap.

As a general rule, allow the saw to cut at its own speed. Any excessive force will be indicated by the driving motors straining and starting to slow down.

band saw

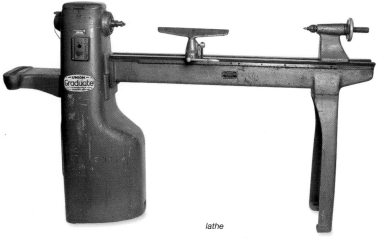

lathe

LATHE

The lathe allows you to accomplish a wide variety of tasks, ranging from the turning of legs, bobbins, bead mouldings and spindles to the copying of handles and decorative roundels or paterae.

Due to the speed and torque at which lathes operate, a lathe with a heavy cast body is ideal for restoration work, as this will counter any vibration. It is essential to take an approved instructional course in lathe work before you start using one as misuse can result in serious injury.

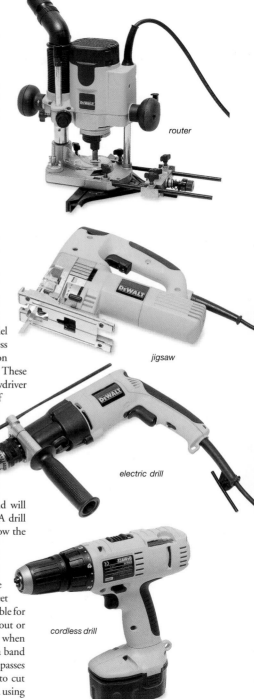

router

router bench

jigsaw

electric drill

cordless drill

ROUTER

The router is an extremely versatile hand tool. Its shaped cutter rotates at high speeds and will, if used correctly, give a clean, even cut. It can also be used with a guide fence or depth stop, and the range of cutters available is immense. Care should be taken in its use: no loose clothing should be worn, hair should be tied back and eye protection should be worn.

ROUTER BENCH

The router bench allows the router to be mounted upside down and so converted into a spindle moulder. The bench should always be used with guide fences and safety guards. The bench can often be dismantled, allowing for convenient storage when not in use.

POWER DRILLS

Cordless and electric drills are both ideal machines for workshop use. While you may sometimes require the use of a more traditional hand drill, such as when undertaking delicate work that may need to be executed one turn of the drill bit at a time, a power drill is one of the few modern tools that is preferred over the old

version. Always buy the best model possible and, in the case of a cordless drill, always have the spare battery on charge ready to be changed over. These drills can also be used with screwdriver heads, although this would, of course, be for more general use and not for fine antique work, since the brass and steel antique screw heads would break if a power drill were used on them. Both types of drill can be used with a variety of bits and will accomplish a multitude of tasks. A drill stand can also be purchased to allow the drill to be used as a pillar drill.

JIGSAW

The jigsaw has a blade with a rise and fall action that cuts through sheet wood with ease. While it is not suitable for fine work, it is ideal for roughing out or cutting shaped templates (patterns) when the pieces are too large to fit into a band saw. Remember that the blade passes through the wood and continues to cut below, so care should be taken when using this tool.

COLLECTING AND STORING WOOD

A supply of suitable wood is an essential aspect of a restorer's workshop, and different kinds must be sourced, collected and properly stored. To the casual observer, such a collection of pieces of wood, salvaged from previous centuries of furniture making, may seem little more than firewood, but to the antique furniture restorer they are a priceless commodity, as without them his or her task would be impossible to undertake.

The aim of every restorer is, wherever possible, to restore a piece of furniture without trace. To do this requires the use of old surface woods and veneers that match the original as closely as possible in colour and grain. Also, when missing mouldings have to be remade, the material used must be of the same type as the original in order to make a good repair.

Two woods in constant demand by restorers are Cuban and Honduras mahogany, which, during the 18th century, were the woods of choice for furniture making. Both are now nearly impossible to buy from any wood merchant, and so any old examples found must be bought and put away until needed. This shows the vital importance of the restorer's "breaker store".

The breaker store, as the name so graphically describes, is a collection of pieces of antique furniture that have been bought not to be restored but to be carefully knocked apart, sorted into the various woods and stacked away for future reuse in the restoration of better pieces. Such an example might be a collection of quarter-sawn oak drawer sides, waiting to be used in the repair or replacement of a missing drawer, or perhaps an old Cuban mahogany table leaf, long ago separated from its table, waiting to be used in the making of a missing bracket foot or to be reshaped with a moulding plane to replace a missing section of top moulding.

The source of breakers is endless, and no opportunity should be missed to scour junk shops, local auctions or even skips. An old Victorian chest bought for very little indeed could provide enough oak

linings, Cuban mahogany and even old locks to pay for itself many times over. Building a comprehensive breaker store can be a lifetime's work, and a useful tip to keep a store expanding is that every time some wood is used from the store, it should be replaced with more wood than

was taken out. Indeed, it is a prerequisite for application to the antique restorers' most senior trade organization, The British Antique Furniture Restorers' Association (BAFRA), that the applicant is able to demonstrate the active building-up of a collection of breakers.

Right: A well-stocked and logically arranged breaker store will supply a restorer with wood to match virtually any restoration project.

The breaker store should be racked and labelled and the woods stored in the various marked sections. This saves both time and effort when searching for a particular piece and enables the restorer to see which, if any, types of veneer are running low or are not represented at all.

Any veneers should be removed from their wood core (see p.28) and stored separately in a veneer store. Any nails and screws should also be removed, partly for potential reuse if they are in good condition and partly as a method of preventing any unnecessary scratching from occurring. The store should be kept

dry but not overly so, as excessive heat will cause the woods to warp and split, creating as many problems as dampness.

While the majority of woods will be old, if an opportunity arises it is a good idea to buy some modern woods, such as walnut, yew or oak for renovating country-made pieces. These should then be professionally cut into boards, stacked so that air can circulate freely between them and allowed to dry and season naturally under cover.

If, however, space will not allow this storage, and modern wood has to be purchased when needed, remember that

it is always better to buy air-dried rather than kiln-dried wood, as the former will be more stable in the long term.

To the untrained eye, a restorer's breaker store may look like a confused jumble of wood. The owner, however, will know all the stock that is there, even wood that was acquired years ago. When a particular grain or surface is needed, the restorer should be able to locate it almost immediately, recalling it from the day it was placed there. Next to tools, an extensive and expanding supply of breakers is one of the most important considerations for a furniture restorer.

Below: *An example of the numerous repairs for which the components of a breaker chest can be used.*

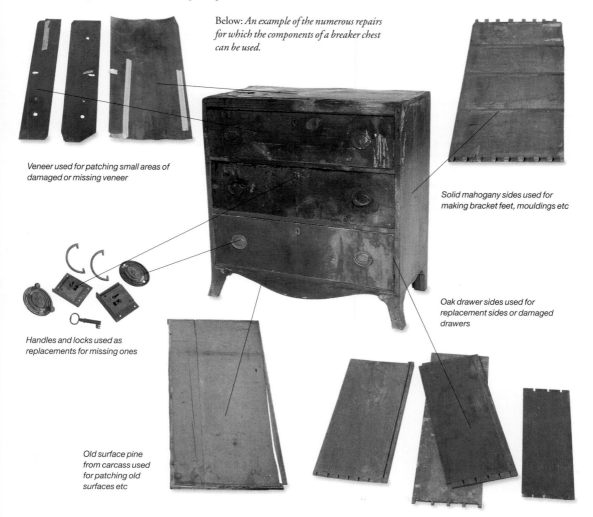

Veneer used for patching small areas of damaged or missing veneer

Handles and locks used as replacements for missing ones

Old surface pine from carcass used for patching old surfaces etc

Solid mahogany sides used for making bracket feet, mouldings etc

Oak drawer sides used for replacement sides or damaged drawers

COLLECTING AND STORING VENEERS

While early furniture was made using solid wood, by the late 17th century the use of veneer was becoming more widespread. Originally cut by saw, by the latter part of the 19th century thinner (and therefore cheaper) veneers were cut by peeling the log, a technique known as "knife cut", which increased their use still further. Whenever possible, a comprehensive store of used and new veneer should be stocked.

Veneers, like breakers (see p.26), are an important commodity for any serious-minded restorer. While good veneer merchants will hold a comprehensive stock of various cuts of veneer, it is still a good idea for the restorer, wherever possible, to compile a separate store in a shed or unused room. This veneer store should include not only new veneers, which may be bought in bundles, often held together with string, but also old surface veneers, which may have been removed from breakers.

With time, the colour of certain woods can alter greatly from their original colour, and for this reason the furniture restorer should aim to collect as wide a range of old surface veneers as possible.

Left: A selection of bandings and stringings, which are often used in veneer work, are useful. They can be purchased from good veneer merchants.

Before being stored, old surface veneers will need to be removed from their core. A damp cloth is placed on top of the veneer and is then heated with an iron. The resulting steam softens the original animal glue, allowing the veneer to be gently eased off. This is done by sliding a flat-bladed knife between the veneer and the core. The old glue should be washed from the back of the veneer with hot water while it is still sticky.

The veneer should then be placed between two sheets of paper and have pressure applied to it. A hand veneer press is ideal for this, but alternatively the veneer can be placed between two flat pieces of wood with weights placed on top. This will allow the veneer to dry flat.

When the veneer is dry, it can be sorted with any other new pieces and then placed in the veneer store. Long lengths should be stored flat on slatted wood shelving, which allows the air to circulate freely. Smaller pieces, which can be used to repair

cross bandings or inlays, can be placed in shoe boxes. The storage shed or room should not be allowed to become too dry, because this will cause the veneers to shrink and split. If possible, a slightly damp and cool atmosphere is best, because this allows the veneers to remain malleable. Laying cardboard on top of the veneer will also stop it becoming too dry and brittle.

Selecting a particular veneer from the store is a task best carried out by two people, one at each end of the veneer bundles, so that they can turn the bundles evenly as they search for the exact match. This method should prevent any unnecessary damage to the bundles. If, however, a veneer develops a split that starts to travel up its length, secure this with a piece of brown parcel tape.

When a piece of veneer has been removed from a shelf, the remaining pieces should be replaced in the same order as they were originally stacked. Failure to do so could result in different veneers being stacked together, which would then make selecting a particular veneer much harder in the future.

Left: Any veneer store should be racked to allow the veneers to lie flat and be easily and quickly identified.

COLOUR AND PATINATION

Without doubt, the two most important aspects to any antique furniture are those of colour and patination. People often think that the two are the same, but in fact both are different, as each term refers to a different aspect of the finish found in antique furniture. It is the glorious colour and surface patination that furniture develops that the buyer and collector both seek. And their presence, or at times their absence, can radically alter the value of a particular piece.

Colour

The colour of a piece is found in the actual surface of the wood. This surface area illustrates how the wood has reacted over the years as many generations of natural light have affected its surface. It is interesting that for numerous reasons two pieces of the same wood, such as Cuban mahogany, can react in different ways. This can depend on the amount of light a piece has been exposed to or how dense a particular grain is. Also, a solid rounded piece, such as a chair upright, will react differently to a flat area, such as a chest top. Veneer will also change its appearance in a different way to a piece of solid wood.

Different woods can also be changed quite markedly over time, for instance kingwood and rosewood are both very purple when first cut and polished, but become a golden colour after many years of exposure. The change in mahogany, which when first polished has a very red tone, ranges from dark nutty brown to light honey colour. It is this variation that makes each piece of antique furniture unique. Unfortunately, this colour can easily be ruined by over-zealous cleaning, which allows chemicals to alter the tones, colours and hues of the wood. It is worth remembering that once altered, the original colour cannot be returned.

Patination

The term patination can best be described as the history of a piece mirrored in its surface colour and shine. Technically, it is caused by generations of oxidation of the polished surface, combined with a build-

Above and below: *These photographs illustrate the inner and outer surface of an 18th-century tea table. The inner surface, which has spent its lifetime closed and protected from the effects of light, has kept the original red colour (top). In contrast, the top of the table has mellowed and, after generations of waxing, has developed a magnificent patinated surface (below). This is an example of mahogany colour and patination at its best.*

up of furniture waxes, natural grease and dust. Its appearance can be altered by many factors, including sunlight, the amount of waxing a piece has received in its lifetime, whether any solvents have been applied and the type of finish originally used when the piece was made. For example, the patination found on a piece of mid-18th-century mahogany, which would have been polished with oil, varies greatly from that found on an early 18th-century piece of walnut, which would have been finished with varnish and wax. While good patination is often present on good pieces of furniture, truly great patination is rare. When it is present, therefore, every effort should be made to maintain it.

VENEERS AND WOOD

It is the sheer variety of the woods and veneers used in their construction that makes furniture, both antique and modern, so pleasing. During previous centuries, as new woods were discovered and imported, it allowed cabinet-makers and designers to explore new techniques and designs utilizing the qualities unique to these woods. The opening up of the world in terms of trade can be directly linked to changes in furniture design over the centuries.

During the 16th century, almost all furniture was still made from solid wood. By the latter part of the 17th century, however, veneer began to play an increasingly important role in furniture making. Some changes in construction techniques followed, and in certain pieces the carcass was now little more than a framework on which to apply the veneer. Dutch, French and Italian furniture-makers experimented with marquetry and parquetry designs, while others began to use native woods such as walnut and elm – all which had formerly been used in the solid – in veneer form to gain the maximum benefit from the beauty of the grain and natural burr patterns. These same burrs, which would have been far too unstable to appear in solid wood furniture (they have a natural tendency to split and twist during seasoning after

Left: *The tools used for cutting and laying veneer are fairly basic and have remained unaltered throughout the centuries.*

construction), could now be cut into thinner veneers and applied on to a stable core carcass of oak.

The first veneers were cut by hand. This was laborious and meant that the veneers were thick and fairy expensive to produce, but as quality furniture was still a luxury commodity, it mattered little. With the use of industrial machinery during the 19th century came thinner and cheaper veneers. These veneers allowed previously expensive woods such as mahogany and satinwood to be incorporated into a wider range of furniture.

How veneers are cut

To slice veneers from a log, the log is mounted in a frame that rotates or slides up and down against a sharp blade. Depending on the way the log is mounted, different sections of the figure in the grain can be displayed to their best effect.

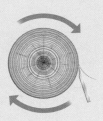

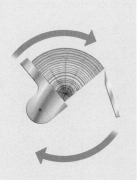

Rotary-cut veneers follow the growth rings in the log as it is unpeeled like a giant roll of paper. They are produced in large sizes.

Flat-cut, or crown cut, veneers are cut parallel to the centre line of the log. Woods with distinct growth lines are best sliced in this way.

Quarter-cut veneers are cut at right angles through the rings. This displays the rays in wide bands, as in quartered oak, with its distinctive silvery "flash" rays.

Rift cut, or comb cut, veneers are cut with the blade offset at a slight angle from the quarter position. This produces a fine parallel grain figure.

Types of veneer cuts

One advantage of using veneers over solid wood, which was quickly appreciated by the cabinet-maker, was that each individual tree as well as each species of tree could produce examples of many different types of patterns. This allowed the cabinet-maker and furniture designer to break up an expanse of wood with patterns and designs that are both unique and highly decorative.

However, although no two pieces of veneer are exactly alike, they can be categorized into broad types, depending on from which part of the tree they come from and their general pattern and form.

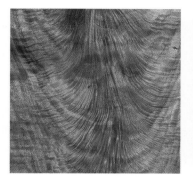

CURL VENEER

A curl veneer is obtained by cutting from the fork of the tree where the trunk divides. It gives a feathering effect, and in woods such as mahogany was highly sought after for drawer fronts and tops. Mahogany curl veneer was particularly popular during the 18th and 19th centuries.

BURR VENEER

The burr is found on the side of the trunk where numerous growths have occurred. Often found near the bottom of the tree, they are sometimes known as burr clusters. Usually only available in small sections, they are unstable until glued to a stable core.

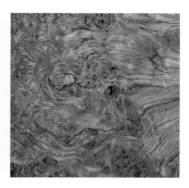

BUTT VENEER

This veneer, as the name suggests, is taken from the root, or butt, of the tree. Dense in grain, it is often wild in figure with much swirling movement.

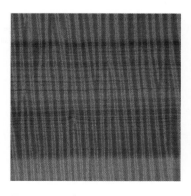

FIDDLE VENEER

This prized veneer was used in the manufacture of violins, hence its name. It has a distinctive stripe, which usually runs at right angles to the grain, and was favoured during the 18th century with mahogany and stained sycamore, known as harewood.

FIGURED VENEER

Not as wild as burr but still with movement, this type of veneer was popular in the making of quarter-veneered tops and bookmatched ends. Various theories abound as to why some veneers are more figured than others, but it is this variety that creates uniqueness.

OYSTER VENEER

The oyster veneer, which is obtained by slicing through the branch to give distinctive rings, was popular during the 17th and early 18th centuries from woods such as olive, walnut and laburnum. It was usually then enhanced with geometric line inlays of box or holly.

Veneer treatments

Although it is possible for veneers to be simply applied in sheet form, it is far more usual for them to be laid in decorative patterns. The range of patterns is fairly small and will often be dictated by the type of cut of veneer and the origin or date of the piece. When these veneer patterns are laid, it is important that the sheets of veneer are selected from the same bundle, and indeed in the same order in which they were cut, otherwise the pattern can seem disjointed.

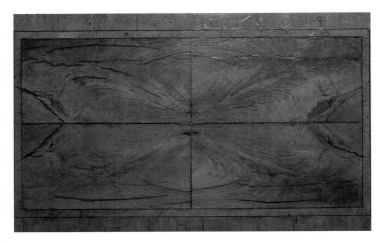

QUARTER-VENEERED

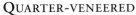

As the name suggests, this is the design where the top is veneered in a quarter pattern radiating out from the centre. The most popular cut used is the figured veneer, although the use of burr is also known. Quarter-veneers were often bordered with further crossbanding to form a frame. During the 19th century, round tops were veneered in numerous curls that radiated toward the centre, but this was known as segmented veneering.

BOOKMATCHED

The bookmatched veneer surface is obtained by taking two subsequent veneer sheets from a bundle, opening them out and laying them next to each other so that they form a counter pattern, rather like the wings of a butterfly. This is done with figured veneer and can be found on the sides or fronts of chests or bureaux, or perhaps on the top of a centre table.

BLOCKED

This technique was used during the 17th century, especially on the ends of marquetry chests. It allowed a patterned centre to be veneered around quickly and meant that odd cuts of a veneer could be used when a pattern would make it difficult to cut around. (Marquetry panels were laid prior to the surrounding veneer being applied.)

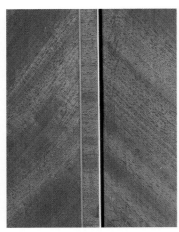

FEATHERED

In this method the veneer is cut and laid at an angle. Although quite rare, it is found on certain 18th- and 19th-century pieces of quality to give a decorative treatment to a door.

SCARF-JOINTED

This technique is used when a straight edge is not possible or desirable, for example when using burr veneers that come in small pieces. While they may be cut straight along the quartered line, the joints connecting the various pieces should remain hidden to give the illusion that each quarter is in fact one piece rather than a number of pieces joined together. A wavy cut is made that should be lost in the swirl of the grain. Over time, the veneer may shrink a little due to seasoning and the joints may become visible again.

Types of veneer

Like solid wood, veneers are affected by the action of light, polish and wax. Indeed, the range of colours found in veneer can be quite marked, and it is these colours, tones and hues that are so readily sought after today by the collector.

Although the types of woods used are numerous, and choice very much depends on the origin and date of the piece, the majority of popular antiques today use the woods illustrated in the following sections.

MAHOGANY

Numerous types of mahogany are available, but the two most commonly used for furniture manufacture during the 18th and 19th centuries were Cuban (*Swietenia mahogoni*) and Honduras mahogany (*Swietenia macrophylla*). With its rich red colour and dense hard grain, this solid wood was ideal for furniture manufacture. When cut into veneer form, the mahogany was highly decorative, especially when the sought-after curls were used in the door panels of bookcases or linen presses.

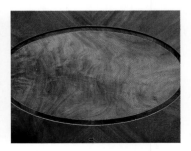

Above: *Cuban mahogany veneer prior to use and polishing.*

Above: *A Cuban mahogany curl veneer panel having mellowed and patinated to a wonderful surface.*

Above: *A George III linen press, c.1790, veneered in well-figured Cuban mahogany throughout and with curl veneer panels.*

WALNUT

European walnut (*Juglans regia*) was widely used for furniture manufacture from the 17th century onward, and by the end of that century its use in veneer form was increasingly fashionable for the finer pieces.

Although indigenous to warmer European climates, such as France, Italy and Turkey, it was also produced in England. The Great Frost of 1709 destroyed most of the European trees, and so its export from France was banned after 1720.

Its use in furniture in veneer form declined during the 18th century, but it become popular again during the mid-19th century. When first polished, it is almost orange, but it will mellow to either a honey colour or a rich nutty one.

Right: A walnut veneer.

Right: A walnut veneer after 300 years of waxing.

Above: An 18th-century walnut-veneered bureau of excellent colour and patination.

ROSEWOOD

This wood comes in two forms: Indian rosewood (*Dalbergia latifolia*) and Brazilian rosewood (*Dalbergia nigra*). During the 18th century, Indian rosewood was more commonly used in the solid in Indian and Anglo-Indian furniture, while Brazilian rosewood was more favoured in veneer form during the 19th century. It is often seen on table tops laid on to a mahogany core. While deep purple when first polished, rosewood mellows to a rich warm tone and on occasion can even become golden brown in colour.

Right: A Brazilian rosewood veneer.

Right: A Brazilian rosewood veneer that has developed a rich colour.

Above: A Regency centre table, c.1815, veneered in well-figured Brazilian rosewood and inlaid with brass.

SATINWOOD

West Indian satinwood (*Zanthoxylum flavum*) originates from the Caribbean islands, while East Indian satinwood (*Chloroxylon swietenia*) comes from southern India and Sri Lanka. The wood was not in demand for furniture making until the mid-18th century. Although it was sometimes used in solid form during the latter part of the 19th century, it was mainly used in decorative veneer form. East Indian satinwood, which can be seen on later 19th-century pieces, is richer in colour than the West Indian variety and often has a characteristic ribbon stripe when the veneer is quarter cut. It is yellow when first polished, but develops a golden rich colour over time.

Right: *A piece of West Indian veneer when first cut.*

Right: *A West Indian veneer that has mellowed and patinated to a golden yellow/orange colour.*

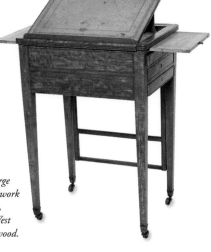

Right: *A George III game and work table, c.1785, veneered in West Indian satinwood.*

OAK

There are more than 300 varieties of oak, but European and English oak are the same species – *Quercus robur*. Until the 17th century, most furniture was made from oak. However, as the century progressed, newly imported woods became fashionable and oak was largely downgraded to either internal carcass work or country-made pieces. When first cut it is a light honey colour, and if quarter sawn it will show its distinctive, silvery, medullary ray figure, but after initial waxing it can become much darker and will continue to darken over time.

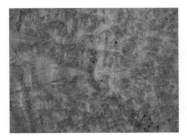

Right: *Oak when first cut, with its light golden colour.*

Right: *With time and generations of waxing, a rich warm tone will develop.*

Above: *An early 19th-century sarcophagus wine cooler veneered in burr oak.*

POLISHES AND GLUES

One of the most attractive features of antique furniture is its distinctive grain patterns. It is the application of polish and waxes that, while helping to protect, feed and nourish the wood, also enhances its appearance. The polishes and techniques used today are nearly identical to those used for generations before, although the restorers of old would have had to make their own polish recipes as well as making all their own glues.

POLISHES

Ever since wooden furniture was first made, its grain has been sealed in one way or another. Waxes were used to burnish the surface, and, during the 17th century, varnishes were applied that helped to protect and enhance the wood. During the 19th century, a new technique was adopted that resulted in a shellac polish, made from the shells of lac beetles, being applied with a cotton and linen pad known as a rubber (see pp.51–52). This sealed the grain, protected the wood and brought out the pattern and figure of popular imported woods such as mahogany, satinwood and rosewood.

The polisher's basic requirements are few. The equipment involves wadding (batting) and linen or other lint-free cloth for making rubbers, a selection of various grades of wire (steel) wool, as well as a wide selection of various brushes and some mutton cloth for buffing surfaces.

The polisher's materials include shellac polish, which can be bought in either liquid form or as shellac flakes to be

Above: *Brushes, polishes and stains are needed for nearly every restoration job. Keep a good selection to hand.*

mixed with spirit (alcohol), and is kept in a glass or plastic bottle. Various coloured pigments to be mixed with water or spirit are needed for tinting or colouring repairs, and stopping waxes, again in various shades, are also needed. The final material is methylated spirits (methyl alcohol), which should be stored in a fire-proof cabinet. All the above equipment and materials can be obtained from a good trade supplier.

One of the main attractions of an antique piece of furniture is its colour and, hopefully, its patinated surface, so great care should be taken whenever polish is applied. The skill of the polisher is to revive a surface by gently removing the perished layers and then rebuilding the surface layer by layer. Work on small areas should be kept as localized as possible so as not to affect the surrounding areas.

Patience and practice are therefore the watchwords. A good eye for colour is also needed to ensure that patches and repairs blend in with the surrounding areas. They should be practically invisible. It is also essential to have an understanding of traditional techniques and materials and to know when to clean a piece and when it is better to leave it alone. Over-zealous cleaning will not only spoil the aesthetic appearance but will almost certainly devalue the piece considerably.

Professionally, a polisher may take many years to learn the craft, and, without doubt, the polisher's role in a workshop is every bit as important as that of the cabinet-maker or restorer.

Above: *Rubbers should be kept in an air-tight jar or tin to stop them drying out.*

GLUES

Until the 15th and early 16th centuries, very little glue was used in the manufacture of furniture. Instead, the joints were held together with pegs or crude, hand-made clout nails. By the 17th century, however, as furniture construction became more complex and designs and styles more adventurous, animal glues were being employed in furniture making.

While new adhesives have been developed over the years, animal glues are still the most frequently used glues in furniture restoration. The sight and smell of the glue pot in any workshop is the same today as it was in the 17th, 18th and 19th centuries, and putting it on the fire or hot plate is still the apprentice's first task every morning.

Three main types of glue are used in the modern workshop: animal glue, PVA (white) glue and cascamite. Each has its own role and will be selected according to the nature of the required join.

Animal glue

This glue is made today as it has been for the last 300 years: animal feet and skin are boiled and the resulting liquid is poured into cold water, causing it to crystallize into small pearls. These pearls can then be mixed with water and allowed to soak overnight, before being heated in a special glue pot to melt them.

Above: Animal glue is applied hot, using a bristle brush.

Above: The three most commonly used glues today (clockwise from top): animal glue, PVA (white) glue and cascamite.

The glue pot (or gesso kettle) is an iron bain-marie pot with an inner reservoir of hot water. The pot is put on a fire or hotplate until the water boils, and it is then allowed to simmer gently, melting the glue ready for use. A top crust will appear and should be scraped off prior to use.

Great care should be taken not to allow the hot-water reservoir to boil dry. Should this happen, the glue will become too hot and its adhesive qualities will be lost. The remaining glue will then have to be discarded and a new batch prepared.

At the end of each day, the glue pot is taken off the heat and set aside until the next day, when it is simply reheated and the glue reused. A pot of glue could be cooled and then reheated day after day, but it is good workshop practice to make a fresh batch of animal glue every week.

Animal glue is ideal for furniture restoration because it allows a certain flexibility in the joints, it can be removed with hot water or spirit (alcohol) and it sets as soon as it has cooled. It can also be watered down to make a size for use on veneers and surfaces when a piece of furniture needs re-veneering.

The disadvantages of animal glue, however, are that it is affected by extremes of heat and cold and that a sharp blow to a joint will cause it to lose its adhesion. If such a break happens, the joint has to be taken apart, cleaned and reglued. Despite these disadvantages, however, no serious workshop would be without its glue pot.

Above: Animal glues are heated prior to use in an iron bain-marie pot. The water reservoir should not be allowed to boil dry.

PVA glue

Another frequently used glue is the more modern polyvinylacetate, or PVA (white), glue. It is bought in liquid form, is easy to use, needs no pre-application preparation and is unaffected by either extreme of temperature. The joint or two surfaces being joined must be brought under pressure when the glue (which is non-reversible) is applied.

When it is either impractical to have a glue pot simmering away all day, or when you are doing a small restoration job that simply does not warrant the time involved in preparing animal glue, versatile and simple-to-use PVA is the ideal workshop adhesive.

Cascamite

For projects needing an adhesive that will help to hold a shape or form, an ideal glue is urea-formaldehyde resin, or cascamite as it is more commonly known. This comes in a powder form and is mixed with water to a creamy paste. Once the glue has been applied, the two surfaces being joined should be brought under pressure with suitable clamps.

Cascamite is a versatile glue: its natural white colour can be disguised by adding coloured pigments to it, and some types are waterproof, which can be useful. The disadvantage, however, is that it is very brittle when set, making it totally unsuitable for joints, because just a knock could shatter the glue bond.

GILT AND STAINS

Gilding and staining are both methods of enhancing and disguising wood to give a better appearance. While stains are used in the main by the restorer to disguise repairs it should be remembered that during the 17th and 18th centuries inferior woods were often stained to give them the appearance of more exotic and expensive ones; for example pearwood was stained black to resemble the more sought after and expensive ebony.

GILT

The use of gilt to decorate and highlight furniture has been a part of furniture making for centuries. The two techniques used are those of oil and water gilding, each of which gives a distinctive look. Some specialist materials and equipment are needed, but the most important ingredients that the gilder requires are patience and skill.

Gesso is a mixture of powdered chalk, rabbit-skin glue and boiled linseed melted in a gesso kettle, and it is used to build up the surface before gilding. A few layers can give a thick, even coat. It can have sand mixed in with it for a textured finish.

Bole is a mixture of clay and water that is available in red, white or blue and is used to form the next layer in the gilding process. Once this is dry, a size of alcohol, rabbit-skin glue and water is applied. The surface is now ready for the gold leaf to be laid gently in place.

The gold used in gilding has been rolled on machine rollers and then hand-hammered into leaves of varying levels of

Above: *During the 17th and 18th centuries metalware on the finest pieces was occasionally fire gilded.*

fineness. It can be bought in a number of different grades, depending on the carat.

Agates are used to pull together joins between the leaves and for burnishing. Originally made from dog's teeth (they are also known as "dog-tooth agates"), they are now made from synthetic materials.

Right: *The tools of the gilder have remained basically the same through the centuries, although modern plastics are now replacing dog teeth.*

Water gilding

Gold leaf cannot simply be laid on to bare wood when water gilding. Bases of gesso and then bole must be applied first, and then the gilt can be laid, evened and finally distressed.

STAINS

The majority of coloured stains are either water- or spirit- (alcohol-) based, although on rare occasions a slow-drying, oil-based stain may be used. They are used to colour in repairs or to help colour out and disguise marks. Some stains can be bought in liquid form, but for the best range of tones and colours you will need to buy stains in powder form, ready to be mixed with spirit or water.

Spirit-based stains, usually mixed with methylated spirits (methyl alcohol), are quick-drying, because the spirit rapidly evaporates in air. This makes them unsuitable for use on large areas, as some areas will dry before others, causing an uneven finish. Spirit stains are usually applied after polishing. If the polish is applied on top of the stain, the spirit in the polish will dilute the stain and lighten the surface colour.

Water-based stains dry more slowly, making them suitable for large areas because they give an even finish. They are generally applied before polishing. One disadvantage, however, is that they can raise the grain, which will then need to be flattened before you can proceed any further. Both spirit and water stains can be thinned after application by adding further spirit/water.

Left: *Stains often have to be tailor-made to suit the job in hand.*

Below: *Stains can be purchased in colour powder form, which are then mixed with a suitable solvent.*

Other stains, such as coloured waxes, are not frequently used in furniture restoration. Their use is generally confined to moderating the colour of a surface slightly after it has been polished.

Stains can be applied by brush, which should be thoroughly cleaned after use with a cloth or by a dowel with some cloth wrapped around the end, known as a swab (see p.54). Alternatively, some polish can be mixed with a small amount of stain and applied not with a rubber but with a fad. This allows the whole area to be slightly tinted, and it overcomes the problem of the spirit base making the colour lighter.

Mixing a spirit-based stain

1 Aways use a clean container and a flat-bladed knife or small teaspoon for mixing stains. Methylated spirits (methyl alcohol) is an ideal spirit liquid mixer.

2 Pour the required quantity of methylated spirits into the clean container. It is better to add powder to liquid rather than liquid to powder, in order to avoid unnecessary wastage. Select the correct powder required for the colour effect desired, and add a small amount at a time.

3 Mix with a clean brush. If a stronger stain tone is needed, simply add further powder. When you have finished with the stain, pour away the unused stain and clean all the utensils and the brush to ensure that the next coloured stain to be mixed is not tinted with any residue from this one.

MOUNTS, CASTORS AND METALWARE

The range of mounts, castors and other metalware is vast and is influenced by the date, style and country of origin. In the past, such items were ordered from the local foundry when needed. Indeed, at times a strong indication of the piece's original maker can be gained simply by studying its original metalware. By the 18th century, the foundries were beginning to publish designs and you can often find their name stamped into a hinge, castor or lock.

Unlike today, when screws, nails and brass fittings are factory-made in their tens of thousands, the brassware and fixings of the previous centuries were all hand-made. Clout nails, which had roughly shaped heads, and hand-made screws, which had off-centre, hand-cut slots, were all works of art in their own right. It is a testament to their quality that, some 300 years after being made, they can be fixed back into their original locations ready to be used again.

As with the breaker store for wood (see p.26), or the veneer store for old surface veneers (see p.28), an equally important part of any restoration workshop is the brasswork store. Any old nails, screws or brassware that are removed from a piece of furniture are kept here for future use. While skilled foundries can make copies of period mounts, castors and galleries (small ornamental railings surrounding the top of a desk, table, etc.), there is still no substitute for the original. Each piece of bespoke brassware was designed for its particular role.

Above: *A selection of metalware dating from the 18th and 19th centuries, including mounts, castors and a section of gallery.*

Left: *A mid-18th-century Louis XV Japanese lacquer commode is richly embellished with ormolu mounts.*

Above: *A selection of 18th- and 19th-century brass castors, which, in spite of years of use, are still in working order.*

During the 18th and 19th centuries, there were two methods of treating brassware once it had been cast to prevent tarnishing: fire gilding and lacquering. Fire gilding was an expensive process usually reserved for the finest mounts, galleries and handles. The process involved mixing mercury with gold, applying it to the metalware and then heating it. The mercury would evaporate and the gold would bind to the metal. This gave a rich, bold finish, but, due to the mercury fumes that were constantly being given off, the life of the mercury gilder was a short one. The second method, lacquering, gave a similiar, if not quite as rich, appearance to fire gilding. Unfortunately, the use of abrasive solvents for cleaning over the years means that the majority of handles have lost their original finishes, but when fire-gilt and lacquered finishes are still largely intact, they should be cleaned with care. For the most part, they require little more than an occasional wipe with a damp cloth.

Blunting a nail

1 *Knocking a large nail into a hard piece of wood, such as oak, can cause splitting. This is due to the fact that the sharp point is acting as a wedge.*

2 *An easy step to counter this is to blunt the point of the nail prior to use.*

3 *Just one or two taps with the hammer are needed to gain the desired effect.*

4 *With the tip now blunted, you can hammer the nail through the wood without it splitting.*

Removing a nail

1 *When a nail needs to be removed from a polished surface, the pliers should not touch the wood as illustrated here.*

2 *The pressure caused by the pliers bearing down on the wood can often cause bruising and marking to the surface polish.*

3 *The preferred method is to place another layer between the pliers and the polished surface. In this instance, a cabinet scraper is being used. Equally acceptable is a thin piece of wood etc.*

LOCKS AND KEYS

The range of types of key is vast, and all workshops should keep as many as possible. Often the more simple lock can be operated with a replacement key that may require little or no alteration. These antique keys can be sourced in many locations ranging from junk shops to local bric-à-brac markets. Replacement blanks, which can be cut to fit locks, are also available and can be sourced from suitable specialist suppliers.

The earliest known locks date from the Egyptian times, around 2000 BC, and the Romans also manufactured and used them. Their use continued through the ages, and by the 14th century locks were not uncommon on English furniture. Indeed, examples from the 14th and 15th centuries are to be found, with their distinctive feature of a flush face plate and sunken movement, both making sure that they could not be prised open. By the latter part of the 15th century, locks were becoming more decorative and their use increasingly widespread. In these periods, it was not only gold and valuables that required safe keeping but equally so correspondence, as a letter swearing allegiance to the wrong party could result in an untimely end.

By the late 17th century, elaborate locks were still in use, but the increasing manufacture of chests and other cabinet furniture meant that a plainer steel lock was being used, often with a simple throw mechanism. As furniture designs became more elaborate, so the need for a more tailored lock increased. Bureaux required angled face plates to mirror the fall, cupboard locks could be designed to

Left: It is important to carry a wide selection of locks and keys salvaged from breaker chests and cabinets.

throw either left or right and, where extra security was required, such as with an escritoire, three- or four-pin locks were used, which made their forcing open very difficult. On continental locks, one often finds a double throw movement, which increases the length the bolt is extended into the lock housing, thereby helping to strengthen the security of the lock.

During the 18th century, brass began to be used on the better-quality locks, although cheaper locks were still made from iron. Their manufacture began to be more elaborate, and, in 1778, a major watershed was reached when Robert Barron designed a revolutionary lever system that, unlike previous locks, which had operated on a ward system and relied on a single tumbler, operated with two tumblers, meaning that in order for the lock to throw open, the tumblers had to be lifted both back and up to a precise height. This lever system still exists in today's locks.

The lock was further developed during the 18th century by Bramah, who, in 1784, patented a system that incorporated a tube-like key with notches on the end that fitted into a lock fitted with springs, meaning that the key had to fit precisely into position in order for the lock to work. Even a slight variation would mean that the lock did not throw, and therefore a very specific key had to be used with each lock. If the key was lost, cutting a new one was a specialist task that required a trained locksmith.

It is rare that a maker would use only one specific lock or key in his furniture making, although one such exception is that of the 18th-century designer and

Right: A selection of Bramah locks with their distinctive patent pattern mark.

furniture-maker Thomas Chippendale. The use of the S key and corresponding escutcheon, while not proved to be exclusive, is widely accepted by academics and collectors alike as a mark of a piece made by Chippendale. Documented examples are to be found on pieces at Brocket Hall, Harewood House and Nostell Priory, all of which are Chippendale commissions.

While general servicing and key replacement should be able to be carried out by a competent restoration workshop, it should be remembered that some locks are very elaborate, and these more complicated examples are better dealt with by a specialist locksmith or restorer.

Above: *During the 18th and 19th centuries, a variety of locks were developed each with a specific role or task to perform.*

Servicing a lock

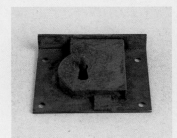

1 Over the years working locks can collect all kinds of debris, such as dust, wax and even insect remains, that will eventually make the lock less efficient. A quick service is all that is needed.

2 Remove the lock and place it flat on a clean surface. Unscrew the retaining screws from the back plate. Take care not to misplace the original screws.

3 Slide the screwdriver carefully between the face and back plate and gently ease it off making sure not to damage either piece. You will now be able to see if there is any debris collected in the lock's workings.

4 Gently remove any debris with a soft brush. Check for any other damage while the back plate is off. If there is any rusting or parts have broken away, restoration must be carried out by a specialist locksmith.

5 When the lock is clean, lubricate the internal workings using a dry silicon lubricant spray. Do not use oil-based lubricants as they will quickly attract dust and cause the same problem over time.

6 Check that the lock works freely, then replace the back plate using the original screws. Check the lock again before placing the lock back in its original position.

Restoration techniques

Tables come in a variety of styles, shapes and forms, often designed with a specific purpose in mind. Depending on their period of commission the material of construction will vary, but often the joints used remain fairly consistent through the centuries. By the nature of their design tables are fairly robust in form, but like all furniture will need restoration to attend to a variety of problems that may arise.

DISMANTLING AND REASSEMBLING TABLES

Although tables come in many styles, their basic construction remains the same and the method required to knock them apart remains fairly consistent. The dismantling procedure must be followed in a logical step-by-step manner, and particular care must be taken to identify the types of joint employed. Failure to do so could result in smashed joints and unnecessary further damage. Once the table has been taken apart, you can inspect the components and carry out any necessary restoration or repair work before reassembling it.

Dismantling the table

This table is a George III, c.1800 drop-leaf Pembroke table made from Cuban mahogany. Over a period of time, its joints have become loose, but before any necessary repair work can be done, the table needs to be dismantled.

MATERIALS AND EQUIPMENT
- chalk or masking tape
- screwdriver
- hammer
- hardwood block
- toothbrush
- rasp

1 Label the various parts of the table, either with chalk or by applying marked masking tape, which will not mark the polish.

2 Turn the table upside down and lay it on a protected workbench. Remove all the screws from the frame, which will release the top.

3 Now unscrew any metal brackets that may have been added to the table in the past to strengthen any damaged joints.

Tip

If a screw is difficult to remove, fit the blade of an old screwdriver into the screw slot, tap the handle firmly with a hammer and tighten the screw slightly. This should break the bond, allowing the screw to be removed.

◁ **4** Examine the construction of the joints to decide the best method of knocking apart without causing further damage.

◁ **5** Disassemble the various components, taking care not to cause structural damage to the joints. Failure to do so will result in smashed joints that will need to be restored prior to the table being reassembled. Use a hardwood block to prevent bruising by the hammer.

6 When separating the side frame from the legs, use the hardwood block again to guard against bruising by the hammer. Direct the blows as closely as possible to the actual joint.

7 Now knock the legs apart from the remaining frame, using the same technique and making sure you put a piece of hardwood between the hammer and the leg to prevent any damage.

8 Remove all traces of glue with a toothbrush and hot water. Where animal glues have crystallized, use a rasp to clean the joint. Take care not to file away any of the tenon, as this will result in a sloppy joint.

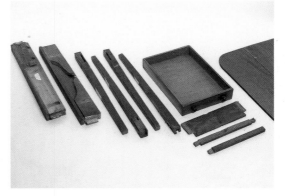

9 Carefully check the various parts of the table once it is dismantled, before carrying out any necessary restoration work.

Reassembling the table

When all the necessary restoration work has been carried out, the table can be reassembled. PVA (white) glue and animal glue are the best adhesives to use.

MATERIALS AND EQUIPMENT
- PVA (white) or animal glue
- sash clamps
- clamping blocks
- hammer
- hardwood block
- masking tape
- drill
- flat-bottomed grain plug drill bit
- grain plug cutter
- mahogany
- chisel
- fine-grade sandpaper
- hand drill
- wood drill bit
- screwdriver
- screws
- flat-bladed knife
- stopping wax
- cloths (rags)
- methylated spirits (methyl alcohol)
- spirit- (alcohol-) based stain
- brush
- rubber
- polish
- wax

1 Glue the front legs and the front frame together. Apply pressure with a sash clamp, using clamping blocks to protect the polished surface, and leave to dry. Repeat for the back legs and back frame.

2 Now complete the table frame by gluing both pairs of legs together, using the bottom rail at the drawer end and the side frame at the other end. Stand the table on a flat, level surface to do this. Make sure that the frame is square by measuring across the diagonal corners. Clamp as before.

3 This top rail is secured by dovetail joints, so it should be glued back into position at this stage. Tap the dovetails into their recesses with a hammer and a hardwood block. If the rail had mortise and tenon joints, it should have been fitted at the same time as the bottom rail.

◁ **4** Before the glue has set, fit the drawer to ensure that the table is square. If the drawer sticks or rubs, you may need to make small adjustments. Leave the glue to dry overnight. When it is dry, remove the clamps.

▷ **5** Beneath the top, there was evidence that the previous screw fixings had been pulled out and the hinge moved to try to get a better purchase. Since the top will be reset in its original position, the old screw holes can be plugged.

6 Follow steps 1 and 2 on p.67 to enlarge the existing screw holes. Cut small plugs of wood to fill them, and then glue the plugs in place.

7 When the glue is dry, use a chisel to level the plugs off flush with the underside of the table, then sand them with fine-grade sandpaper. There is now a smooth surface for the screws to be set into.

8 Now turn the top upside down and put it on the protected workbench. Put the frame back in the correct position. Since the old holes have been plugged, drill pilot holes to locate the positions of the screws.

◁ **9** If you are using the old screws, screw them into the new holes. If you are using replacements, check that they are the right length and will not go through the table top and mark the surface.

▷ **10** Using a flat-bladed knife, fill the screw holes made by the metal brackets removed earlier with stopping wax in a similar colour to the mahogany.

11 Stain the repairs to match the wood. Wash the surface off with methylated spirits (methyl alcohol). Charge a rubber with polish and revive the surface. Apply wax and buff the wood to a warm lustre.

Left: *Reassembled and polished, the table has been restored to its former glory and is ready to give many more years of service.*

POLISHING AND COLOURING

The term "polishing" is used to describe the overall method of filling the grain and enhancing the figure of any piece of wood using shellac polish. The vast majority of polishing work today is commonly known as French polishing, which involves the use of shellac polish combined with oil – often linseed oil – and applied to the wood with a linen rubber.

Within the history of antique furniture, however, there are two very distinctive methods of finishing: varnishing using oil or spirit varnishes, and French polishing, which was introduced only in the 19th century. Both methods create distinctive appearances, and it is the effects of light, oxidation and time that make these polished and waxed surfaces so sought after by today's collectors.

The principles involved in polishing a new surface or repolishing an old surface remain the same: numerous thin layers are built up to form a combined surface. When completed, the polish should have a translucent quality that allows the colour and figure of the wood beneath to be seen. On occasion it may be necessary to tint the polish in order to adjust the final colour. This method of colouring is different from staining with spirit, water or oil, which is the process by which the actual wood tone is changed rather than simply colouring or tinting the polish.

When removing polish from a piece of furniture, it must be done a layer at a time to minimize any damage to the colour and surface of the piece. When the damaged areas have been carefully lifted, further polish can again be applied, a layer at a time, until the required surface appearance is obtained. If too much polish is applied the surface will have a treacle-like appearance; if too little polish is used the grain in the wood will look open and "hungry", resulting in a blotchy effect once the surface has been waxed.

French polishing

Prior to the early 19th century the methods of finishing furniture were mainly the application of varnishes or oils such as linseed and various wax compounds. These were usually applied, often by brush or cloth (cotton rag), after the grain had been sealed with ground brick dust or pumice powder. They served to protect the wood and could be burnished to a soft lustre finish.

In 1820 a new practice, imported from France, came to favour. It was the use of shellac, which comes from the shells of the lac beetle. The shellac, which was dissolved in spirit, was applied layer by layer, giving a hard, glossy finish. Over the years, and with the application of wax, the hard, glossy surfaces mellow, and depending on the style and period of the piece, the surface finish can range from hard and glossy to a soft, almost matt appearance.

MATERIALS AND EQUIPMENT
- wadding (batting)
- linen
- polish
- fine wire (steel) wool
- methylated spirits (methyl alcohol)
- soft cloth (cotton rag)
- shellac
- linseed oil
- clear beeswax

Left: *This Regency table has become severely damaged on its polished surface and must be repolished.*

MAKING AND CHARGING A RUBBER

A rubber is an essential tool for applying a French polish finish and is easy to make. All you need is some wadding (batting) or plain unmedicated cotton wool and a square of linen or similar lint-free cloth. The rubber acts in the same manner as a sponge, absorbing a quantity of the polish (known as charging), which is squeezed out on to the surface being polished when you apply pressure to it. A rubber can also be used to apply a stain to wood.

▷ **1** Lay a 15cm/6in long piece of wadding (batting) on the centre of a piece of linen the size of a large handkerchief.

2 Fold the ends of the linen inward and grasp them in the centre of your palm.

3 With all the outer edges gathered together, twist the ends of the linen to form a tail.

4 The rubber is complete when the tail is completely twisted. For a smaller, more intricate, polishing job, make a smaller rubber to suit.

◁ **5** To charge the rubber, open out the linen to expose the wadding, then pour a small amount of polish on to the wadding. With practice, you will be able to judge the correct quantity. Note that if the rubber is too dry it will not run smoothly over the surface; if it is too wet it will simply lay the polish on the surface.

▷ **6** Refold the linen around the wadding. Squeeze the tail to apply pressure to the wadding, to force the polish through the linen. The more you tighten the tail, the more polish will emerge. After polishing, you can store the rubber for another day.

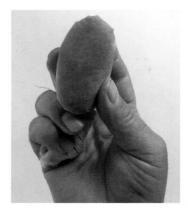

▷

APPLYING THE POLISH

If the damage to a surface is extensive, it will have to be stripped back with methylated spirits (methyl alcohol) before repolishing, as shown here. New wood is polished in much the same way, except that the grain is first filled with pumice and polish, then sanded flat with very fine or broken down sandpaper.

Once the rubber has been charged, the polish can be applied. This process takes time, and the finish must be left overnight for the polish to harden before it can be buffed to a high sheen or cut back to produce a matt finish.

Tip

When polishing with a rubber (step 3) the idea is to "body up" or fill the grain. This is done by first applying the polish in straight continuous strokes along the grain (below top). The polish is then applied in circular motions (below centre) and finally with wider figure of eight movements (below bottom).

1 Remove the old polish and wax surface with fine wire (steel) wool and methylated spirits (methyl alcohol).

2 Once the old polish and wax have been removed, wash off the surface with a soft cloth (cotton rag) and methylated spirits.

3 Polish the surface using a rubber and shellac (see Tip). Linseed oil can be dripped on to the surface to help lubricate the rubber. This technique, known as "bodying up", fills the grain. Leave for at least 24 hours to harden.

4 When the polish has hardened, cut it back lightly using fine wire wool and working in the direction of the grain. Use light strokes to remove any raised nibs of polish. This also produces a higher gloss finish.

5 Finally, apply a coat of wax. Use light strokes as the polished surface will still be delicate. Allow to stand for a week before use to allow the polish to fully harden.

Right: *When polished, the scratches become invisible and the table has an even, soft sheen that should last for years.*

Waxing

All antique furniture will require waxing during its lifetime. Waxing feeds, protects and nourishes the wood. It is the combination of waxes with natural grease and oxidation that forms the surface patination that is so desirable. Over the generations, various types of wax have been used, with workshops producing their own secret recipes.

One of the most common misconceptions is that the more frequently a piece is waxed. the fuller the finish will be. Over-waxing will result in smeary surfaces, since wax softens wax.

The only remedy for this is to remove all the wax and begin afresh. It is far better to wax at sensible intervals and apply only a very thin layer. Use only natural wax-based products.

MATERIALS AND EQUIPMENT	
• clear wax	• soft cloths (cotton rags)
• soft brush	• brush

WAXING A FLAT SURFACE

1 Apply a thin layer of wax using a soft cloth (cotton rag) impregnated with the chosen wax. Never apply too thick a layer, as this will simply make the rubbing up more difficult and time consuming.

2 Even out the wax using a soft brush. Take care not to mark the surface and make sure you work along the direction of the grain. Use long, steady strokes, working from one side of the surface to the other.

3 Allow the wax to harden for a few minutes, then buff the surface vigorously with a soft cloth, working in the direction of the grain. Finally, use a clean cloth to give the surface a final burnish.

WAXING A CARVED SURFACE

1 Due to the nature of the hollows and relief, it is better to apply a thin coat of wax with a soft brush, making sure that it is neither too hard nor too soft.

2 Allow the wax to harden for a few minutes, then gently burnish the carving with a soft brush. This will remove any surplus wax and even out what remains.

3 Finally, buff the highlights using a soft cloth (cotton rag). Mutton cloth, which is available from most trade suppliers, is ideal for this role.

Staining

Paints and varnishes adhere to the surface of the wood, but stains penetrate it, changing its colour permanently. For this reason, stains are favoured by the restorer. They can enrich dull-looking wood or change the colour of new wood so that it blends in with the rest of the piece of furniture. This bureau has had a new piece of wood added to it that must be stained and polished so that it matches the rest of the piece.

MATERIALS AND EQUIPMENT

- spirit-based (alcohol-based) stain
- cloth (cotton rag)
- wooden dowel
- fine brush
- rubbers
- polish
- methylated spirits (methyl alcohol)
- soft brush
- wax

Tip

Spirit-based (alcohol-based) stains, thinned with methylated spirits (methyl alcohol), are the best stains to use, because they dry very quickly. However, they are harder to obtain and more difficult to use. This is because they can leave obvious overlap marks. Solvent- and water-based stains are available ready mixed and are easier to apply.

1 Use a spirit-based (alcohol-based) stain mixed to match the colour of the furniture. For a small area like this, wrap a piece of cloth (cotton rag) around one end of a dowel and use this to apply the stain to the new piece of wood. If staining a large area, use a brush to apply the stain. Continue until the colour is even, then leave to dry.

2 Check again that the stain is even. If necessary, add another layer, or draw in the grain with a fine brush (see p.55). When you are satisfied with the colour of the dried stain, charge a rubber with polish and apply a layer to the stain, and also to the rest of the bureau to blend in the stained area (see pp.51–52). Allow the polish to dry.

3 Cut back the polish with a rubber charged with a little methylated spirits (methyl alcohol). The new wood should now be indistinguishable from the old.

4 Use a soft brush to apply a thin coat of wax to the new wood, and the rest of the piece of furniture, to give a soft, even sheen. Leave to dry.

Above: *Now stained and polished, the new wood blends seamlessly with the old.*

Graining

During the late 18th and early 19th centuries, rosewood was imported from India, South America and the West Indies for use in the manufacture of furniture. It was an expensive wood, and so only the finest pieces of furniture were made from solid rosewood; other pieces were made from beech, which was a hard-grained, easily workable, cheap native wood. The beech was "grained" with a paint finish to give the appearance of rosewood. Over time, the areas of graining wear away, revealing the beech underneath, as has happened with this Regency chair. In this case, it is necessary to simulate the rosewood graining while also giving it a patinated, antique look. The techniques for distressing are varied and include using smooth stones, fine wire (steel) wool and homemade tools. These should be practised and perfected before use.

MATERIALS AND EQUIPMENT
- light brown spirit-based (alcohol-based) stain
- fine brushes
- screwdriver
- rubber
- polish
- dark brown spirit-based stain
- wax
- cloth (cotton rag)

Above: *An area of the graining has worn away on the chair leg to reveal the beech wood underneath.*

1 Apply a base coat of a light brown stain mixed to match the base colour of the rest of the chair (see p.54). Leave to dry. Charge a rubber with polish and apply a thin layer.

2 Apply a dark brown stain mixed to match the grain of the simulated rosewood, using a fine brush to replicate the pattern. If no residue of graining is left, use a piece of patinated rosewood veneer as a pattern.

3 When the graining is dry, distress the graining effect using a screwdriver, if necessary, to match the original. Give it another rubber of polish to seal in the effect, then wax the chair using a cloth.

Above: *The grained beech chair, on the right of the picture, now looks very similar to the solid rosewood chair on the left. Both these chairs are dining chairs, made c.1810.*

REPAIRING CARVING

Carving as a form of decoration on furniture has been in existence since medieval times, but by the 17th century its use was becoming more widespread.

When restoring or replacing carving, it is important to select a similar-grained piece of wood. It is often advisable to make an initial test cut with a carving tool to ensure that the wood is suitable to work with. This is because some wood will have a grain that is too "wild", which means that you may tear rather than cut the wood. Alternatively, the wood might be too soft, which could result in the wood simply crumbling when being carved and unable to keep a crisp edge.

Carving a damaged bracket

During the 17th and 18th centuries, carved and shaped legs had brackets, or ears as they are commonly referred to, that were applied separately rather than being part of the leg. As a result, if the animal glue perished, the bracket could become detached and even lost.

This table had lost a bracket from one of its swing legs, so the leg needs to be removed and a replacement bracket made. A profile of the carving on the other swing leg bracket needs to be taken so that it can be used as the basis for the new carved decoration, which can then be stained and polished to match the other legs.

MATERIALS AND EQUIPMENT
- tenon saw
- Cuban mahogany
- spokeshave
- animal glue
- modelling clay
- mallet
- indelible ink
- marker pen
- carving tools
- screwdriver
- fine brushes
- bichromate of potash
- polish
- pumice powder
- cloths (cotton rags)
- rubber
- colour
- fine wire (steel) wool
- wax
- large soft brush

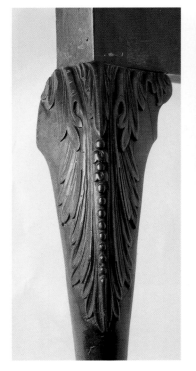

△ **1** Cut a profile bracket out of Cuban mahogany and shape it with a spokeshave. It should be similar to the missing bracket but slightly larger to allow the carving to be undertaken, otherwise it will end up too small. Glue it into place.

△ **2** To obtain the correct profile of the missing carving, lay a piece of modelling clay over the matching bracket on the other swing leg. Tap it lightly with a mallet, then gently peel it away.

3 Turn the clay over and use your thumb to cover the profile of the carving with indelible ink. Then lay it gently on the replacement bracket to leave the outline of the carving on the wood.

4 Remove the clay then thicken the outline with a marker pen, making sure the lines flow into the carving on the rest of the bracket.

◁ **5** Having established the outline of the carving, remove the groundwork using grounders. This technique, known as grounding out, establishes the depth of carving.

◁ **6** When the outline of the carving has been set, carve the detail into the relief, using either veiners or modellers. There should be no need to clean up the carving, as the razor sharpness of the tools should give a perfect finish.

◁ **7** Reattach both swing legs to the table and round off the sharp edges of the new bracket using the shank of a screwdriver or some similar tool.

▷

Carving a damaged bracket...continued

8 In its natural state, mahogany is a red colour, but over the years it patinates to a brown tone. To mimic this colour, apply bichromate of potash, which, being a chemical stain, reacts with the tannin in the wood to turn the natural red tone into a more suitable brown.

9 Apply the polish with a brush, painting it on evenly. The idea is just to fill the grain, so do not use too much, otherwise streaks and runs may occur.

10 Put some polish on a cloth (cotton rag) and sprinkle some fine pumice powder on it. Use this to work the polish into the grain. Do not round over the edges or break through highlights to reveal wood.

11 With the grain filled, use a rubber to apply further polish mixed with some colour until the bracket tone blends in with the leg and matches the original bracket (see pp.51–52).

12 After the polish has hardened, cut it back with fine wire (steel) wool, then wax the bracket (see p. 53).

Right: After the bracket has been polished and waxed, it will look original. It is worth noting the amount of distressing on the bracket you have taken a profile from and trying to mirror it on the replacement. However, be careful not to overdo this and give the bracket a "fake" look.

Carving small pieces

The previous technique covered replacing a completely missing carved section, piece or bracket; on occasion, however, you may need to replace only small pieces of carving. The method or technique used for this is different to that of replacing a complete section, because your aim is to fill in the small areas that are missing with pieces of wood, and then to carve them to match the original. The pieces cannot be carved and then glued into place, as the detailed carving needs to be flowing and the replacements undetectable. This carved foliate bracket has many sections of leaf and vine missing.

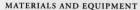

MATERIALS AND EQUIPMENT
- mahogany
- fine-bladed fret saw
- animal glue
- carving tools
- fine brushes
- stain
- polish

1 Hold a new piece of mahogany against one of the missing areas and roughly sketch out the profile in pencil.

2 Use a fine-bladed fret saw to cut the wood to the approximate size. Repeat steps 1 and 2 for all the other missing pieces.

◁ **3** Glue the pieces into place and leave them to dry. Draw in the outlines of the missing pieces to give a guide for carving, although the majority of the work will be done by eye.

◁ **4** After roughing out the outlines, carve the chosen shapes and patterns. Use tools that are razor sharp, otherwise the new pieces may break off. Should this happen, glue them back into position. Finally, add the details, matching the original carver's style.

Above: *When completed, the newly carved areas should be stained and polished to match the rest of the bracket. The highly carved surface demands that a fine brush be used for both techniques.*

REPAIRING TOPS

The top is subject to more general wear and tear than other areas of a table, especially if they are used for meals or children draw at them. Scratches, dents and stains are commonplace, and other problems that can frequently occur with table tops are warping, splitting and damaged decorative edges. Fretwork galleries are particularly vulnerable. By using the correct restoration techniques, however, it is possible to make good all of these defects and to bring a damaged top back to the condition it was in when the table was made.

Restoring a damaged table edge

This Cuban mahogany Georgian tripod table is missing a section of its decorative edge. A new piece of wood needs to be cut, glued in place and shaped to fit, before being stained and polished to match the table top. This technique can be used on all moulded edges, including pie-crust tops.

MATERIALS AND EQUIPMENT

- screwdriver
- mahogany
- jigsaw (saber saw)
- tenon saw
- chisel
- PVA (white) glue
- spring clip
- plane
- carving tool
- spokeshave
- fine-grade sandpaper
- brush
- stain
- rubber
- polish

◁ **1** Remove the table top from the frame by undoing all the screws (see p.46). Turn the table top upside down and lay it on a protected surface. Put a piece of mahogany, slightly thicker than the decorative edging, underneath the top, and draw around the edge with a pencil. Slide the mahogany farther out by an amount slightly greater than the width of the decorative edging, and draw another curved line.

2 Cut the mahogany along the pencil lines using a jigsaw (saber saw), then turn the table top right side up again. Cut through the damaged edging on either side of the missing area with a tenon saw.

3 Remove the damaged wood underneath the missing edging with a chisel. Continue working until you have a flat, level surface.

4 Check that the piece of mahogany fits in the allotted space. Apply PVA (white) glue and secure it with a spring clip. Leave to dry, then remove the spring clip.

5 Plane the mahogany down until it is level with the rest of the edging. Make small strokes to avoid damaging the table top.

6 The inner ledge on the table must be shaped with a suitable carving tool. Again, avoid damaging the polished mahogany.

7 Use a spokeshave to shape the curve along the edge of the top. It is easier to obtain a more delicate shape with a spokeshave than a plane.

8 Smooth the top of the restored area with fine-grade sandpaper. Fold a small piece of the sandpaper in half and hold it with your thumb and forefinger for accuracy.

Above: *Once the detailed shape of the edging has been formed with sandpaper, stain (see p.54) and polish (see pp.51–52) the repaired edging so that it is invisible.*

Repairing a rule joint

The rule joint is commonly found on drop-leaf tables. It allows for a leaf to be raised and supported along its length. On occasion, it can become damaged, as shown here, where part of the rule joint has broken away, allowing the hinge to be seen from the top. This could have been caused by the leaf having been raised too high, putting too much pressure on the hinge and joint.

MATERIALS AND EQUIPMENT
- tenon saw
- mahogany
- PVA (white) glue
- spring clip
- chisel
- fine-grade sandpaper
- fine brush
- stain

1 Trim away the damaged area of moulding with a tenon saw. Cutting the ends at angles will help to disguise the repair when it is finally polished.

2 Cut a piece of mahogany to the length of the gap and a little wider, and glue it in place. Clamp it using a spring clip, which is ideal for this type of small repair, and leave to dry. Remove the clip.

3 Shape the wood with a chisel and fine-grade sandpaper so that it continues the lines of the existing wood, otherwise the flap may not open properly. Stain it to match the existing moulding.

Drilling out damaged screws

The photograph shows a very common problem: after the screws had been put into this card-table hinge, their heads were filed flat to remove the slots. The flap of this table needed routing out, which meant that the screw heads had to be drilled out so that both hinges could be removed.

MATERIALS AND EQUIPMENT
- centre punch
- hammer
- drill
- metal drill bit
- screwdriver
- long-nose (needle-
- nose) pliers
- Cuban mahogany
- PVA (white) glue
- chisel

△ **1** First hammer a centre punch into each screw head as accurately as possible.

▷ **2** Drill out the heads of the screws taking care not to drill the actual holes in the hinges any larger than they already are. This will leave countersunk holes, which will be filled by the replacement screws when the hinges are refitted.

3 Using a small screwdriver, carefully ease the hinges clear, being careful not to bend the flaps of the hinges out of shape.

4 Removing the hinges will expose the shanks of the screws, which will still be embedded in the table edge. Drill small holes on each side of, and as close as possible to, the embedded screw shanks.

5 To remove the screws, insert a pair of long-nose (needlenose) pliers into the freshly drilled holes, grip the shank of each screw in turn and pull it out.

◁ **6** The holes must be filled before new screws can be inserted. Cut wedges of Cuban mahogany and glue them into the holes. Trim them flush with a chisel when dry.

Right: *Once the table has been repaired, the hinges can be refitted.*

Repairing fretwork

The illustration shows the damaged open-fret gallery from a Georgian silver table, c.1760. The silver table, as the name suggests, would stand in the drawing room and have the silver tea service placed upon it. Such tables were designed to be elegant and often had open-fret galleries, made from three layers of veneer for strength.

The gallery on this silver table has been damaged and small areas have broken away and been lost. As much as possible of the damaged fretwork will be glued back into place, and the missing areas within this will be filled with pieces from a new section of gallery made specially for the purpose.

MATERIALS AND EQUIPMENT

- superglue
- paper
- wood block
- clamping blocks
- G-clamps
- Cuban mahogany
- band saw
- toothing plane
- cascamite glue
- pigment
- brushes
- hammer
- veneer pins (tacks)
- pincers
- plane
- drill
- wood drill bit
- fine-bladed fret saw
- paring chisel
- tweezers
- fine file
- spirit-based (alcohol-based) stain
- polish

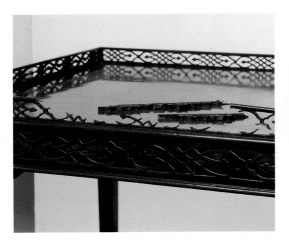

△ **1** The first step in the restoration process is to put back as much of the damaged work as possible, gluing it into place with superglue. The quick-drying nature of this glue allows the gallery to be held in the correct position while the glue sets.

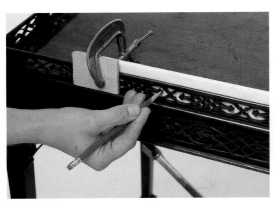

2 To make a new section of gallery for the repairs, wrap a piece of paper around a long block of wood and then use G-clamps and some clamping blocks to hold it against a section of gallery that matches the damaged area. Draw the outline of the fretwork very carefully. Release the clamps and blocks and remove the piece of paper.

3 Cut three lengths of Cuban mahogany with a band saw, roughly the length of the damaged fret area, and, using a toothing plane, plane one side only of two lengths and both sides of the third length. This will aid the purchase of the mahogany when the three layers are glued together.

4 Cut one length into pieces of the same length as the width of the remaining two lengths. These will be the inner core pieces that will give strength to this new section.

5 Cascamite glue, while suited to this job (see p.37), could show as a white line on this gallery, so add a small quantity of pigment to the powder prior to mixing it with water.

6 Coat the planed side of one length of mahogany with cascamite glue then place the short pieces on top to form a second layer. Coat these short pieces with glue.

7 Place the second length on top, planed side down. Tap in two or three small veneer pins (tacks) to prevent the newly formed laminated section slipping when it is clamped up.

8 Place paper strips on either side of the section then put clamping blocks in place. The paper will ensure that any excess glue does not bind the two together. Clamp the section under pressure and leave to dry. The pressure must be even along the whole length.

9 Remove the clamps and blocks, then pull out the veneer pins with pincers. Failure to remove the pins could result in damage to the fret saw when the fret is being cut.

10 Place the gallery in a vice and plane the long edges level with a jack plane.

11 With the laminated section now ready, glue the paper template (pattern) made in step 2 on to it.

▷

Repairing fretwork...continued

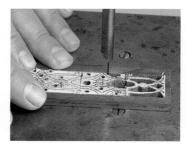

12 Drill holes in each area that needs to be fretted out. This will allow the fret saw blade to be put into position.

13 Using a fine fret blade, cut out the open fret, following the design. Work slowly and take great care not to spoil the work already done. Scrape off the remains of the template.

14 Before restoring the glued fretwork, cut any splintered breaks flush using a sharp paring chisel. To protect the fragile fret, place a block of supporting wood behind it.

15 Cut out the sections from the new fret needed to fill the gaps with a fret saw, and carefully insert and glue them in place.

16 Use a fine file to smooth the edges flush where the old and new pieces join, taking care not to alter the open-fretted shape.

17 Repeat until all the damage is repaired. Finally, stain and polish the new portions of fret to match the existing gallery.

Right: *With the fretwork restored, stained and polished, this silver table can once again be returned to the drawing room of the large country house from where it came.*

Filling screw holes

Over the years, a piece of furniture may be subjected to a number of repairs that relied on brackets or reinforcing plates being screwed on. During restoration, these will be removed, leaving the screw holes behind. Fortunately, it is easy to fill these holes with wooden plugs.

MATERIALS AND EQUIPMENT
- masking tape
- drill
- flat-bottomed grain plug drill bit
- grain plug cutter
- wood
- PVA (white) glue
- chisel
- fine-grade sandpaper
- brush
- stain

1 Mark the required drilling depth on the flat-bottomed grain plug drill bit with some masking tape (see Tip), then drill a hole larger than the old screw hole.

2 Use a grain plug cutter to cut a plug from matching wood, making it slightly longer than the hole's depth. Glue it into the hole.

3 When the glue has dried, pare off the projecting portion of the plug with a sharp chisel, then sand it smooth.

Above: *The finished repair is now ready to be stained.*

Tip

If a drilled hole must not penetrate all the way through a piece of wood, it is vital to know how far you can drill before this will happen. First ascertain the required depth of the hole by holding the drill bit against the edge of the wood, then mark this level on the drill bit with a piece of masking tape. When drilling into the wood, stop as soon as the masking tape touches the surface. The hole will then remain invisible from the other side.

Correcting a warped card table

A dry level of humidity is the most common cause of warping. The flaps of veneered card tables, and other types of flap-over or drop-leaf table, are more prone to warping than frame tables for two reasons. First, they are usually relatively thin (for ease of handling), and second, they are free-standing, secured to the base only by their hinges.

The flap of this mahogany card table is significantly warped. Fortunately, the veneer has not split, which means that the core material can be removed from the baize-covered side, and then replaced with a new, flat MDF (medium-density fiberboard) interior. Finally, a new baize cover can be added without disturbing the veneered upper surface.

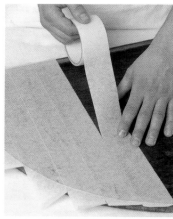

1 Lever the edge of the baize away from the table with a flat-bladed knife. Grip the baize firmly with both hands and pull it off with one continuous movement. Unscrew the hinges linking the flap to the table.

2 Place the flap, veneer side up, on a protected workbench. Cover the surface with strips of masking tape. This will hold together the veneer, banding and stringing on this side until a new core is inserted.

3 Cut a semicircle of padded packaging to fit the flap. Secure it over the veneered side with masking tape for extra protection. Turn the flap over so that the stripped side is uppermost.

4 Immerse a cloth (cotton rag) in a bowl of water, then lay it over part of the banding. Place a hot iron on the damp cloth and press down for a few seconds, then remove the iron and cloth. The steam will soften the glue holding the banding on to the core. Take care not to scorch the banding.

5 Slide a flat-bladed knife under the banding while the glue is still malleable, and lift a section of it from the flap. The stringing should be removed at the same time. Continue steaming and lifting sections of the banding and stringing until all of it has been removed.

6 Tape the pieces of the banding and stringing together on to a board in the same positions that they occupied on the table. This will ensure that they can be replaced in the correct order.

◁ **7** Scrape any remaining baize from the flap with a scraper. In this case, evidence of a previous, and unsuccessful, restoration can now be seen. This method involved removing strips of wood from the warped upper layer, flattening the table, then replacing them with new wood.

▷ **8** Scribe a line around the edge of the flap, just inside the banding's position, with a marking gauge. Turn the flap over, remove the padded packaging, then turn it back again. Removing the packaging will allow the flap to lie completely flat.

Tip

To hold a table flap securely while working on it, you will need to make several holding blocks, which can be screwed down over the table flap on to a chipboard (particle board) base. Make each block 5–7.5cm/2–3in long from softwood that is at least 12mm/½ in thicker than the flap. Cut a rebate (rabbet) along the length of each block to the depth of the flap, producing an L-shaped end profile. Drill two screw holes in each block. Place the flap on the chipboard base and clamp the edges down by screwing the blocks to the base, using chipboard screws (see right).

9 Place the flap on a piece of chipboard (particle board) and press it flat with both hands. Place holding blocks (see Tip) at regular intervals around the edge.   ▷

Warped card table...continued

10 Select a suitable thickness of MDF (medium-density fiberboard) for the core. Remove sections of the flap to this depth, leaving borders to support the router.

11 Cut away the supporting border with a gouge. Take great care not to cut too deeply because you risk damaging the veneer from the underside.

12 Level the surface with the iron from a smoothing plane, continuing until it is completely smooth.

13 Place the flap on the MDF and draw around the outline. Remove the flap and cut along this line with a jigsaw (saber saw).

14 Mark another line on the MDF that approximately matches the width of the banding, and cut along this line. Check that the MDF core fits the cut-out area of the flap, sanding it to fit if necessary.

15 Spread PVA (white) glue over the cut-out area of the flap, then insert the MDF. Place the flap between two pieces of wood and use G-clamps to apply even pressure. Leave to dry.

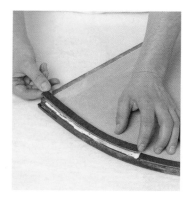

◁ **16** Remove the clamps and wood, turn the flap over, and remove the masking tape from the veneered side. Place the flap, veneered side down, on a protected workbench. Apply PVA glue to the edge of the flap and replace the pieces of banding and stringing.

▷ **17** Reattach the flap to the table and lightly polish the banding with shellac polish. This will remove any traces of watermarks that may have occurred when it was being steamed off.

18 Scrape any remaining baize from the rest of the table with a scraper and then use the scraper to fill any damage with wood filler. Protect the banding and stringing by covering them with masking tape.

19 Cut a piece of baize about 7.5cm/3in larger all around than the table and flap. Apply glue to the surface and lay the baize on top. Working from the centre, push the baize outward to remove any creases.

20 Cut the baize with a utility knife so that it lies flush with the inner edge of the banding. Take care to cut in an even line and not to cut the banding. Leave to dry. Remove the protective masking tape.

◁ **21** Seal the baize by heating a tooling wheel on a hotplate and then running it around the edge of the baize. Apply a firm, even pressure from start to finish.

Below: *MDF (medium-density fiberboard) does not warp easily so there should be little or no risk of this card table warping again.*

Tip

If a surface is warped only slightly, it may be best to leave it as it is. To assess the extent of a warped surface, hold a long ruler alongside it. As a guide, if you can fit your little finger between the ruler and the surface, restoration is required.

Repairing a split pedestal table

Splits to table tops occur either along the grain of the wood or, if the top is made from glued boards, along the joints. Splits along the grain should be secured with butterfly keys, but splits along the joints can simply be reglued and clamped.

The top of this mahogany pedestal table is made from two pieces of wood. The original glue that held them together has perished, allowing the pieces to separate and a gap to appear. The task of regluing is a relatively simple procedure – most of the work involved in this instance lies in dismantling and reassembling the table.

MATERIALS AND EQUIPMENT

- screwdriver
- chalk
- flat-bladed knife
- drill
- flat-bottomed grain plug drill bit
- chisel
- plane
- PVA (white) glue
- sash clamps
- clamping blocks
- hammer
- hardwood block
- mahogany grain plug cutter
- fine brush
- stain
- rubber
- polish
- cloth (rag)
- wax

1 Place the table upside down on a protected workbench, and unscrew the column and legs from the bearers. Mark the position of each separate section of the table top with chalk.

2 Remove the decorative mahogany plugs that cover the steel screw heads on the rim, lifting them out with a flat-bladed knife. Place these in a labelled container for safe keeping (see Tip).

3 Unscrew each of the screws on the rim, remove them and place them in the container. Lift the rim from the underside of the table top and place it to one side.

Tip

Small fittings and fixtures are easy to lose, and if you are working on more than one piece of furniture, you may waste time trying to attach the fitting from one piece of furniture to another piece. To prevent this from happening, always store small parts from a single item of furniture – such as plugs, screws, hinges and knobs – together in a labelled container, such as a glass jar, a can or a box with a lid. Keep them on your workbench for easy access.

4 Drill out the wooden plugs that cover the screws in the bearers with a flat-bottomed grain plug drill bit, but stop short of the heads of the screws. Remove any remaining wood above the screw heads with a chisel.

5 Loosen the screws on the bearers with a screwdriver, remove them, and put them in the container. Lift the bearers from the top and place them to one side.

6 Set a plane to the shallowest cut possible and go over the mating edges of the top once or twice. Apply PVA (white) glue and clamp the pieces together. Tap down raised edges with a hammer and a hardwood block.

7 Cut new plugs from a piece of mahogany using a grain plug cutter. Taper one end of each plug with a chisel, making small grooves down the length at the same time.

◁ **8** Screw the bearers back on to the table top with the original screws. Apply some PVA glue to the holes, then tap the plugs into the holes to cover the screws.

▷ **9** Pare the plugs down with a chisel until they are flush with the bearers. Avoid scratching the bearers as far as possible.

Left: *The gap between the sections of the top has gone. This technique is quick and simple, and produces a very satisfying result.*

10 Mix a water- or spirit-based (alcohol-based) stain to match the bearers (see p.39) and apply with a brush. When the stain is dry, attach the column and legs. Charge a rubber with polish and apply a light layer to the table top (see pp.51–52), then add a wax finish (see p.53).

PROJECT: DROP-LEAF TABLE

During the early 18th century, the drop-leaf table became a favoured type of dining table. This design allowed the table to be stored with its flaps down when not in use, thus saving space. Nowadays, such tables are still extremely popular, and are particularly practical in modern homes where space may be at a premium. Unfortunately, like so many other items of antique furniture, drop-leaf tables may have led hard lives and may now suffer from all manner of ills, ranging from stained and discoloured tops to severe damage to the structure.

ASSESSING THE PROJECT

This George II table, constructed in c.1745, is made from dense red walnut, and its distinctive moulded pad-foot design suggests that it is Irish in origin. It has sustained a sprung glue line in a panel on the flap, which reveals a previous dowel-joint repair. There is also veneer and bracket damage to the carcass, several pieces of one of the feet are missing, and one of the swing legs has broken off and been lost, so needs to be replaced.

The top
- split top, previously repaired with dowels
- watermarks and scratches

The legs
- foot broken
- one swing leg missing

The carcass
- veneer missing
- damaged shoulder
- broken brackets

Repairing the top

Damp caused the glue joining two sections of the table top to perish, producing a split. This revealed an earlier dowel-joint repair. As the dowels were in good condition, they can be incorporated into the new repair. The table top is also marred with various marks and scratches, so the surface needs to be revived thoroughly.

MATERIALS AND EQUIPMENT
- screwdriver
- chalk
- pliers
- plane
- PVA (white) glue
- sash clamps
- long clamping blocks

1 Place the table upside down on a protected workbench. Remove the fixing screws and put the frame and legs aside. Now the frame is off, the pivoted gates and the remaining swing leg can be lifted clear.

2 Unscrew the flap hinges from the main section of the table top. Mark the underside of the top with chalk so that you can tell which flap belongs on which side. Remove the dowels with pliers.

3 Place the main section of the top in a vice and plane the split side of the wood until smooth. Do not take off too much wood, as this will reduce the width of the table. Repeat for the other split side.

4 Apply PVA (white) glue along both split edges, replace the dowels and secure with sash clamps and long clamping blocks. Leave to dry, then remove the clamps.

▷

Repairing the carcass

The carcass, or framework, of the table is in good order and does not need to be knocked apart and reglued. There are, however, missing areas of veneer and two brackets that have fallen off and need refitting. One of the shoulders is also damaged. Due to the untouched patination of the piece, only old surface breaker veneer is used for repairs.

REFIXING THE BRACKETS

One of the brackets had broken cleanly off and needed gluing back in place. A second bracket had also fallen off, due to damage at the point where it joined the table leg. This meant that the shoulder needed to be repaired before the bracket could be refixed in place.

MATERIALS AND EQUIPMENT
- toothbrush
- PVA (white) glue
- spring clips
- tenon saw
- red walnut
- plane
- G-clamp
- clamping blocks
- gouges
- fine-grade sandpaper

◁ **1** Remove the old glue from both the brackets that have fallen off using a toothbrush and hot water. Refit the bracket that sits under the missing veneer patch using PVA (white) glue. Use spring clips to hold the bracket in place while the glue dries.

◁ **2** Turning now to the leg with the damaged shoulder, use a fine tenon saw to cut away a small section to allow for an inset patch to be applied. Cut a new section from a piece of red walnut.

▷ **3** Glue and clamp the new piece of wood in place. When it is dry, plane it flush with the shoulder. There is now a level surface to which the bracket can be reattached.

4 Glue the original bracket back into place, sandwiching the new wood between the leg and the bracket. Clamp until dry. Using a shaped gouge, pare away the excess wood to give a smooth, flowing repair.

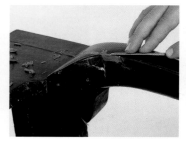

5 With a smaller, rounded gouge, carve the moulded edge to the bracket, so that the repair is unnoticeable.

6 Finally, finish the repair by using fine-grade sandpaper to remove any rough edges. Take care not to mark the polished areas.

REPLACING THE VENEER

Parts of the decorative veneer on the base have become detached and been lost after the animal glue has perished. The veneer must be replaced with matching old surface veneer.

MATERIALS AND EQUIPMENT

- old veneers
- toothing plane
- utility knife
- PVA (white) glue
- clamping blocks
- G-clamps
- fine-grade sandpaper

◁ **1** Select a few possible replacement veneers for the missing patch on the frame, and hold them by the table to see which provides the best match to the original, paying attention to grain and colour.

◁ **2** Before laying the new piece of veneer, remove all traces of the old animal glue with the iron from a toothing plane. Scrape away only the residue of old glue without altering the actual groundwork.

◁ **3** Trim the veneer to roughly the correct size and glue it into position. Make sure that the veneer is laid with the grain pattern running in the correct direction, otherwise the repair will be all too obvious.

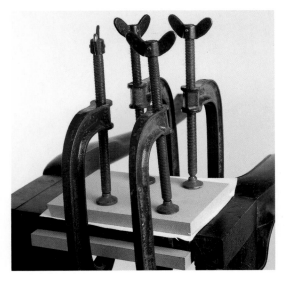

◁ **4** Place some paper on top of the veneer and then put clamping blocks on either side of the damaged frame. Clamp securely with G-clamps and leave to dry. Remove the clamps and blocks.

5 Hold one of the clamping blocks at an angle against the front of the frame to form a cutting base. Use a utility knife to trim the veneer, following the outline of the carcass, then sand the edge.

▷

Repairing the legs

This table is unusual because it has two different styles of leg. The four fixed corner legs are cabriole with shaped lozenge feet. One of these feet has been damaged and needs to be rebuilt. The other two legs, which are swing legs, are turned club legs with small pad feet. They are attached to the frame by swing gates, which support the table flap when it is lifted. One of these swing legs in now missing and a replacement must be made to match the remaining leg.

MATERIALS AND EQUIPMENT	
• red walnut	• lathe
• steel straightedge	• callipers
	• turning tools
• tenon saw	• dividers
• drill	• fine-grade sandpaper
• wood drill bit	

TURNING A NEW LEG

Legs on tables seldom break into pieces, but if they do sustain substantial structural damage, they must be replaced, as it is important that they are extremely robust and strong. One of the swing legs on this red walnut drop-leaf table had been removed, then misplaced, so a new leg needs to be turned and fitted.

1 Cut a piece of red walnut slightly larger than the final size of the leg. Mark the centre of each end of the block by drawing two diagonal lines with a steel straightedge. Cut a shallow groove along one of the lines at one end with a tenon saw.

2 Drill a hole in the centre of each end, about 1cm/⅜in deep. The tail stock of the lathe will be housed in the end with just the hole, and the head stock will sit in the end with the groove and hole.

▷ 3 Secure the block of walnut in the lathe and make a shallow cut with a tenon saw where the turned area will finish and the square section will begin.

4 Use callipers to measure the widest part of the other swing leg so that you can turn the new leg to the correct size.

5 Turn the wood until you achieve the required diameter. Check the size of the new leg frequently with the callipers so that you do not inadvertantly remove too much wood.

◁ **6** Use dividers to transcribe the various dimensions of the decorative foot area from the other swing leg.

7 Turn the decorative parts of the leg with a very small gouge. Always remove less wood than you think you should, at first, and take measurements regularly from the existing leg.

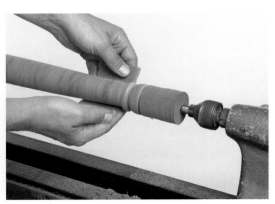

8 Once you have turned the leg to the correct shape, use fine-grade sandpaper to finish off and smooth it. Remove the leg from the lathe and cut it to shape.

▷

CUTTING THE MORTISE

The newly turned leg now needs to have a mortise cut into the square section that was left at the top. The leg can then be attached to the tenon on the gate.

MATERIALS AND EQUIPMENT	
• set (carpenter's) square	• fine-grade sandpaper
• utility knife	• bichromate of potash
• mortise gauge	
• G-clamp	• fine brushes
• clamping blocks	• water-based stain
• mortise chisel	
• cardboard	• rubber
• tenon saw	• shellac polish
• PVA (white) glue	• screwdriver
• sash clamp	

1 Detach the other swing leg from its gate and place the new leg side by side with it. Using a set (carpenter's) square and a utility knife, mark across the shoulder lines.

2 Set a mortise gauge to match the width of the tenon on the swing gate that belonged to the missing leg.

◁ **3** Mark the correct position of the mortise between the scribed shoulder lines on the new leg.

▷ **4** Clamp the leg securely to the workbench, using a clamping block to stop any possible bruising to the leg, and cut out the mortise with a mortise chisel of a suitable size.

5 Take a cardboard template (pattern) of the top of the other swing leg, then mark out this shape on the top of the new leg. Cut away the unwanted wood with a tenon saw.

6 Apply PVA (white) glue to the end of the original tenon and insert it into the newly cut mortise. Clamp the joint under pressure using a sash clamp and clamping blocks. Leave the joint to dry then remove the clamp and blocks.

7 Sand the top of the leg with fine-grade sandpaper, wetting the wood in between sandings to raise the grain. The benefit of this is that the grain will not be raised when a water-based stain is applied.

8 Apply a thin layer of bichromate of potash to the entire new leg. This will change the reddish tone of the walnut to a more suitable brown.

9 After selecting and mixing a suitable water-based stain, apply this to the leg to match the other swing leg.

10 Charge a rubber with shellac polish and apply it to the leg. Distress the leg to match the other swing leg.

REPAIRING A FOOT

One of the pad feet has various broken and missing parts, which, due to their damaged edges, cannot simply be reglued, and so must be replaced. A template (pattern) must be taken of an undamaged foot, so that the extent of the repairs can be determined and the new pieces of wood cut to size.

MATERIALS AND EQUIPMENT	
• profile gauge	• carving tools
• mount card (stock)	• bichromate of potash
• red walnut	• fine brushes
• tenon saw	• polish
• PVA (white) glue	• cloth (cotton rag)
• spring clips	• fine pumice powder
• utility knife	
• block plane	
• coping saw	
• rasp	

◁ **1** Draw the outline of an undamaged foot using a profile marker on a piece of stiff mount card (stock). This will be used as a template (pattern) to repair the damaged foot.

▷ **2** Place the damaged foot on the template and mark along the broken edges. This will indicate what shape and size the new pieces of red walnut need to be. Cut the pieces of walnut to a suitable size to fill the gaps. Glue them into place one piece at a time so that you build up the profile. This gives extra strength.

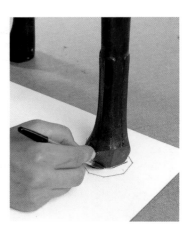

81

Repairing a foot...continued

3 Using a tenon saw, trim the excess wood away, but remember that the foot has yet to be shaped, so allow enough extra thickness for the shaping to be done.

4 To get the profile of the undamaged foot's chamfer, make a second template, this time of the bottom of the complete foot. Cut it out and place it on the bottom of the foot being restored and mark the outline.

5 Using a small block plane, follow the mark on the bottom of the foot to obtain the correct chamfer. Remember to work with the grain and not across it, as this would result in the wood tearing.

◁ **6** Use a coping saw to create the shape of the actual pad foot. The coping saw allows an angled cut to be made, which helps to shape the foot.

▷ **7** Use a rasp to shape the desired profile. Do not to go too far, because there is still a raised lozenge foot to be carved.

8 By cross-referencing to an undamaged foot and by following the line of the raised decoration on the original leg, sculpt the moulding on the restored foot.

9 Give the new wood a thin coat of bichromate of potash – a chemical stain that will react with the tannin of the wood and change the walnut's natural red tone to a more suitable brown.

10 Brush on a thin layer of polish to fill the grain of the walnut. Put some polish on a cloth (cotton rag) and sprinkle some fine pumice powder on it. Use this to work the polish into the grain, blending the old and new surfaces.

Reassembling and polishing

With all the structural work now complete, the restored table can be reassembled. The old screws will be used again and as all parts were labelled prior to disassembling, and the correct position of the top marked, this should be a fairly straightforward process.

MATERIALS AND EQUIPMENT
- screwdriver
- methylated spirits (methyl alcohol)
- cloths (cotton rags)
- fine brush
- stain
- rubber
- polish
- wax

1 Turn the table top upside down and place it on a protected workbench to avoid any unnecessary scratches or marks. Screw the frame and legs back in place, as well as the gates for the two swing legs, using the original screws.

2 Put some methylated spirits (methyl alcohol) on a cloth (cotton rag) and cut back the surface, taking care to remove as little of the original surface as possible.

3 Stain the repairs (see p.54). Polish the table (see pp.51–52) and when it has hardened, wax and burnish it (p.53).

Above: *The restored table, with its brackets refitted, missing veneer replaced, foot repaired, a new swing leg attached and the surface revived and polished, can be fully enjoyed and appreciated once again.*

PROJECT: SOFA TABLE

The term "restoration" can cover a multitude of necessary techniques, ranging from simply removing a scratch or two, to having to undertake what may seem, at first glance, a lost cause. This George III sofa table, c.1810, is veneered in rosewood and is of good quality and colour. Originally designed to stand behind a sofa, it had stood under a bedroom window and been used as a dressing table. Unfortunately, a pair of reading glasses left on the table during a very hot day had magnified the sun's rays on to the curtains (drapes), which caused them to ignite. This led to the back edge of the sofa table catching fire, which completely destroyed some areas and damaged others.

ASSESSING THE PROJECT

The cross-banding along the front and top edge has been completely destroyed, and the damage has gone through to some of the groundwork beneath. The drawer front of one false drawer has been lost, along with the turned rosewood knobs. On one of the flaps, the heat of the fire has caused the glue line in the mahogany core to spring apart. Fortunately, the veneer has separated cleanly with no tearing occurring. A few pieces of cross-banding are missing from the edge. General wear and tear had caused some of the legs to become loose, so these needed to be detached, cleaned off, and reassembled, and some veneer and stringing were missing from the base pedestal.

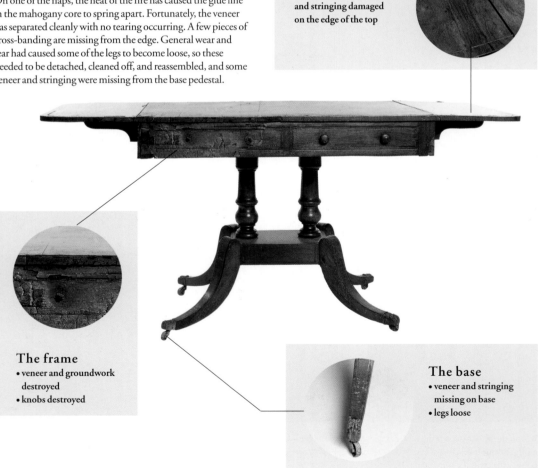

The top
- flap split along glue line
- veneer, cross-banding and stringing damaged on the edge of the top

The frame
- veneer and groundwork destroyed
- knobs destroyed

The base
- veneer and stringing missing on base
- legs loose

Repairing the top

The heat of the fire has caused the glue line in one of the flaps to perish, causing a split. The fire has also caused extensive damage to the edge of the table – the veneer, banding and stringing. The first task is to repair the split, after which the damaged edge can be restored.

SECURING THE FLAP

The damage to the flap appears worse than it is. It has split along the glue line, so can simply be reglued and clamped.

MATERIALS AND EQUIPMENT
- screwdriver
- toothing plane
- PVA (white) glue
- sash clamps
- clamping blocks
- G-clamps

◁ **1** Turn the table upside down on top of a protected workbench. Remove the base, then unscrew and remove the frame. Separate the twin flaps from the top. Store all the screws carefully for reuse (see p.72).

2 Separate the two parts of the split flap carefully. Remove the residue of glue from the glue line with the iron from a toothing plane, which will also provide a key for the new joint line.

3 Glue the two parts of the flap back together. Apply sash clamps and clamping blocks to keep the join under pressure, and use G-clamps to keep the join flat, using paper to prevent any sticking.

▷

85

REBUILDING THE EDGE

The edge of the table top has suffered some serious damage. The groundwork, veneer, stringing and cross-banding have all been destroyed and must be replaced. Luckily, the damage has not gone any further than the stringing inlay, so a line exists at which the new veneer can join the undamaged parts, with the stringing hiding the joint.

MATERIALS AND EQUIPMENT
- router
- guide fence
- softwood
- tenon saw
- PVA (white) glue
- masking tape
- plane
- chisel
- toothing plane
- old veneer
- boxwood stringing
- clamping block
- utility knife
- fine-grade sandpaper

1 Using a router fitted with a guide fence, remove some of the damaged area of veneer and groundwork, but leave a rebate (rabbet) into which sections of new groundwork can be glued.

2 Cut pieces of softwood to replace the routed-out section of groundwork. Apply PVA (white) glue and fit these in place, securing them with masking tape while the glue dries.

3 Plane the new groundwork flush with the front edge. Remove the remainder of the veneer up to the stringing line with a chisel. Scrape the planed groundwork with the iron from a toothing plane.

4 Select a piece of old surface veneer that best matches the original veneer, and glue it over the old and new groundwork. This will ensure that the edge retains its original strength. Lay the replacement stringing at the same time to ensure a tight-fitting joint.

5 Trim the replacement banding flush with the edge (see step 5 on p.77) then sand with fine-grade sandpaper. Use more of the old surface veneer to repair the damaged areas of the cross-banded edge, following the same method.

Repairing the frame

Half of the front of the frame has been reduced to charcoal. Although it appears to be beyond repair, the careful application of new groundwork, the selection of a good match for the new veneer and the construction of some new drawer knobs will make a complete repair possible.

REPLACING THE GROUNDWORK AND VENEER

The charred wood must be removed before a replacement piece can be added and the new veneer applied.

MATERIALS AND EQUIPMENT
- router
- guide fence
- smoothing plane
- tenon saw
- pine
- PVA (white) glue
- G-clamps
- clamping blocks
- plane
- rosewood
- utility knife
- chisel
- scratch gauge
- boxwood strip
- hammer
- sash clamp

◁ **1** The damaged areas of the drawer front must be repaired before the drawer can be re-veneered. Set a router to a suitable depth to cut away the charred veneer and groundwork. To maintain an even depth of cut, clamp a guide fence to the frame for the router to run on.

2 Go over the routed area with the blade from a smoothing plane. This will level the surface and key it so that the glue can achieve a good grip. Measure the area and and cut a piece of pine slightly larger than this.

3 Spread glue over the routed area, then place the new piece of pine in position. Clamp it with G-clamps and clamping blocks and leave it to dry. When it is dry, remove the clamps and blocks, then plane the pine flush with the top and bottom edges of the frame. ▷

Replacing the groundwork and veneer...continued

4 Select a piece of old surface rosewood that matches the colour and grain of the original veneer as closely as possible, and then steam or cut the veneer off.

5 Place the frame in a vice. Starting with the top drawer rail, make matching angled cuts on the original and new veneers with a utility knife. Glue the new piece in place.

6 Remove the remaining areas of damaged veneer by lifting them gently away with a large chisel.

7 Glue a piece of the previously selected veneer on to the damaged false drawer front. Place a clamping block on top to ensure that no blistering occurs, then apply a G-clamp.

8 Remove the frame from the vice. Replace the piece of veneer that is laid at right angles over the joint between the two false drawer fronts. This is set proud to imply that the drawer fronts are real.

9 In preparation for adding the inlaid boxwood strip, cut a groove using a scratch gauge set at the correct width. Keeping the cutting blade sharp ensures a clean trench.

10 Cut a boxwood strip that matches the original in shape and colour. Soak it in hot water. Lay the strip in the groove, then push it into position with the back of a hammer.

11 Glue more pieces of the selected veneer over the damaged end panel. Clamp these into place using a sash clamp and a clamping block.

REPLACING THE KNOBS

Two new knobs must be turned to match the old ones. It is important to take several measurements from the existing knobs to ensure that the new ones are exactly the same shape.

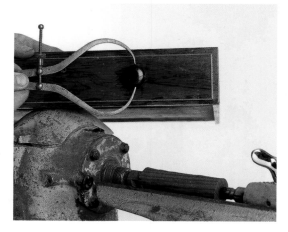

◁ **1** Measure the diameter of an original knob with some callipers. Solid rosewood can be difficult to source, so if you cannot find any rosewood, choose well-figured walnut, which makes a suitable alternative.

MATERIALS AND EQUIPMENT
- callipers
- rosewood or walnut
- lathe
- turning tools
- dividers
- fine-grade sandpaper
- drill
- wood drill bit
- screws

2 Turn the new piece of wood to a diameter marginally larger than the dimension set on the callipers. Make frequent checks because if you remove too much material, you will have to start again.

3 Using some dividers, and referring back to the original knob for guidance, mark the approximate positions and sizes of the various parts of the knob, such as the handle, neck and back.

4 Having scored the various marks, trim the knob to the correct length. Remove the tailstock from the lathe, release the turned wood from the headstock and place it in the chuck.

5 Using the original knob as a pattern, turn the new knob to the same size and shape.

▷

Replacing the knobs...continued

6 Finish off the turned knob by giving it a light sanding with fine-grade sandpaper. Repeat steps 2 to 6 to make the other knob.

7 Find the location for the knobs by using dividers to transfer the dimensions from the undamaged drawer to the repaired one.

8 Drill the drawer front and fit the knobs dry. Do not glue; it is better to stain and polish them first.

Repairing the base

The legs have become loose due to general wear and tear. They need to be removed, cleaned off, then reattached. There are also some patches of veneer and stringing missing on the pedestal.

MATERIALS AND EQUIPMENT

- screwdriver
- chalk
- hammer
- hardwood block
- toothbrush
- PVA (white) glue
- sash clamp
- clamping blocks
- rosewood veneer
- utility knife
- chisel
- masking tape
- steel straightedge
- boxwood strip
- fine brush
- stain
- methylated spirits (methyl alcohol)
- rubber
- polish
- cloth (cotton rag)
- wax

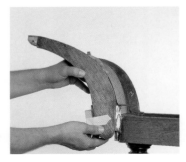

1 The legs were joined to the table by dovetail tenons, which had been reinforced by metal brackets. Remove these brackets, making identifying marks with chalk.

2 Knock the legs apart using a hammer and a hardwood block to ensure that no damage is caused to the legs.

3 Clean off all the old adhesive with a toothbrush and hot water. Reglue the legs, securing them with sash clamps, and replace the metal brackets.

4 After selecting a piece of rosewood veneer that is a close match for the original veneer, hold it over the damaged area and mark around it with a sharp utility knife. Remove the old veneer from within the marks with a sharp chisel.

5 Glue the veneer into place, securing it with masking tape. Use a steel straightedge and a utility knife to cut a rebate (rabbet) in the new veneer for a boxwood strip. Cut a boxwood strip that matches the original in shape and colour. Soak it in hot water.

6 Glue the boxwood strip into the rebate, pushing it into place with the back of a hammer. When the glue has dried, trim the inlay flush using a sharp chisel, taking care not to damage any polished areas. Reassemble the table.

7 To finish, apply a matching stain to all the replacement areas of stringing. Stain other new repairs, including the knobs, and refit them.

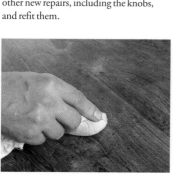

8 Finally, wash the surface with methylated spirits (methyl alcohol). Polish the table (see pp.51–52) and when it has hardened, wax and burnish the surface (see p.53).

Above: *With the fire-damaged areas removed and replaced with old surface veneer, and the entire table's surface revived, polished and waxed, there is no indication of the sorry state it was in before restoration began.*

GLOSSARY

animal glue Also known as scotch glue and traditionally used from the 17th century onwards.

astragals Glazing bars on cabinet furniture, forming a geometric pattern.

bain-marie A pot containing hot water in which another container, holding animal glue, gesso or bole, for example, can be gently heated.

banding Decorative inlays of veneer that are used for aesthetic effect. They can be either long-grained or cross-grained and on earlier pieces can be joined to give a chevron effect, known as herringbone.

blister A bubble that forms on a surface when part of the veneer has become detached from its core.

blooming The name given to the white marks left on a polished surface that has been water-damaged or chilled.

bole A clay-like substance that is used in the gilding process.

boulle Also known as buhl, this is the use of fine brass inlay inset into tortoiseshell or ebony backgrounds.

bracket foot A square foot which might have a shaped profile on the inside. The foot most commonly used during the 18th century.

breaker A piece or a collection of pieces of furniture used in the restoration of another item of furniture.

bun feet A ball type of foot favoured during the 17th century and replaced by the bracket foot in the 18th century.

butterfly key A butterfly-shaped piece of wood used to secure and hold splits. It is inset into a piece so that the grain runs at right angles to the main wood. Also known as a dovetail key.

carcass The actual framework of a piece of furniture. Depending on the period, this would be either in the solid or veneered.

cascamite A glue used when forming laminates or shape work. It is very strong but also brittle.

cock beading Thin strips of decorative beading often found around drawer fronts.

colour The tone or shade that wood develops over time.

conservation To maintain a piece by undertaking as little work as possible so as not to alter its present or original form (*see* restoration).

core The moulded shape on to which veneer or mouldings are applied.

cornice The top of a carcass piece of furniture often decorated with dental mouldings, cross bandings or a pediment.

cross-grain mouldings Wood applied to a softwood backing and planed to a moulded profile, applied to a carcass for aesthetic reasons. Introduced during the 17th century, they are more decorative than long-grain mouldings.

Cuban mahogany Mahogany imported from Cuba during the 18th and 19th centuries and the preferred wood for quality furniture. It is densely grained and red in tone when first polished.

cutting gauge A tool fitted with a small blade that is used across the grain to cut a groove. Often used prior to fitting boxwood lines.

de-nibbing The removal of dust that has combined with polish to form small raised nibs on a surface after polishing. This is done by lightly using fine wire wool in the direction of the grain. The surface is then waxed.

dental mouldings Small rectangular pieces applied to a cornice and resembling square teeth. Popular during the mid-18th century.

dovetail saw A fine-bladed saw used for cutting accurate and delicate dovetails.

escutcheon The brassware used in conjunction with locks for both aesthetic and protective reasons.

fading/fad Filling the grain in wood with a mixture of polish and pumice powder. The cloth with which it is applied is known as a fad.

fire gilding A mixture of gold and mercury applied to a metal base and heated until the mercury evaporates and binds the gold to the metal. Favoured during the 18th century; used on the mounts and handles of the finest pieces.

French curve A kidney-shaped scraper used on concave curves.

French polishing Using shellac polish, which is usually applied with a linen and wadding (batting) rubber.

fret A lattice-like decoration, in which open fret is pierced and blind fret is applied to a solid background.

gauge sticks Two lengths of stick which are held together and used to check the equal diagonal measure of a frame to ensure it is square.

gesso A plaster-like substance that is used in the gilding process.

graining Using surface stains and colours to mimic the grain of a solid piece of wood. Favoured during the early 19th century.

Honduras mahogany Mahogany imported from Honduras during the 18th and 19th centuries and favoured for carcass construction.

kickers Strips of wood applied to the inside carcass of a chest, running along the top of the drawer linings, to stop the drawers tipping forward when extended.

linings The name given to the sides and often the bottom of a drawer.

long-grain mouldings Mouldings planed from one length of wood along the grain and applied to a carcass for aesthetic or structural reasons.

marquetry Inlays of decorative scenes.

marriage Two parts of a piece of furniture that started life separately but have now been brought together. Such an example would be a bureau bookcase in which both halves would have started life with another part.

mortise The hollow housing part of a mortise and tenon joint, which is the most widely used joint in furniture construction.

mortise gauge A marking tool that has a small steel point and is used along the grain to mark the shoulders of a mortise.

overloe A shaped block used in conjunction with sandpaper.

parquetry Inlays of geometric patterns.

patera A round or oval, raised decoration often found on cornices or the tops of legs. Can also be used in veneer form.

patination This refers to the build up of waxes, natural greases and dust that over numerous years combines to form a desirable finish on a surface.

pediment Found on top of a carcass and, depending on the period, can be arched, broken-arched or swan-necked in shape.

piecrust The name used to describe the shape of a top usually applying to a tripod table. The top, as the name suggests, looks like the top of a pinched pastry pie top.

plinth The platform base on which a carcass will sit.

PVA glue Polyvinylacetate glue, also known as white glue. Ideal for day to day use.

reeded decoration A raised decoration of parallel, tapering lines, usually found on chair and table legs.

reeds Raised dome-shaped decoration applied along the length of a surface.

restoration To undertaken any necessary work to return a piece as near as possible to its original form but retaining its integrity (*see* conservation).

revive a surface The action of attending to any minor damage or surface oxidation of a polished surface while not repolishing the whole top.

rubber Wadding (batting) wrapped in linen, which is used to apply shellac polish.

runners The strips of wood attached to the bottom or sides of a drawer on which the drawer will run. Sometimes also found as part of the carcass.

scratch box A workshop-made tool that allows parallel reeds to be scratched on a leg (*see* reeded decoration).

shellac Polish that is obtained from the shellac beetle.

skiver Leather taken from sheep. Not as good quality as cow hide.

splay feet A shaped bracket foot that is splayed in profile. Favoured during the late 18th century.

spring clip A workshop-made cramping device made from upholstery springs. Ideal for securing awkward shapes.

stains Usually bought in powder form and mixed with water, spirit or oil depending on the intended use.

stringing Thin lines of inlay, usually of ebony or box, which were used for both aesthetic reasons and as protective edges.

tenon The protruding part of a mortise and tenon joint, which is the most widely used joint in furniture construction.

twist When wood bows in two directions.

warp When a piece of wood has bowed along its length or width.

FURTHER INFORMATION

British Antique Furniture
Restorers' Association (BAFRA)
Rushbrook House,
Benville Lane, Corscombe,
Dorchester DT2 0NN
UK
Tel: 01939 210826
Email: headoffice@bafra.org.uk
Web: www.bafra.org.uk

British Antique Dealers'
Association (BADA)
20 Rutland Gate
London SW7 1BD
UK
Tel: 020 7589 4128
Fax: 020 7581 9083
Web: www.bada.org

Association of Art and Antique
Dealers' (LAPADA)
535 Kings Road
Chelsea
London SW10 0SZ
UK
Tel: 020 7823 3511
Fax: 020 7823 3522
Web: www.lapada.co.uk

Association of Restorers
8 Medford Place
New Hartford
NY 13413
USA
Tel: (315) 733–1952
Fax: (315) 724–7231
Web: www.assoc-restorers.com

Art and Antique Dealers' League of
America, Inc. (AADLA)
PO Box 2066, Lenox Hill Station
New York
NY 10021
USA
Tel: (212) 879–7558
Fax: (212) 772–7197
www.artantiquedealersleague.com

The National Antique & Art
Dealers Association of America, Inc.
220 East 57th Street
New York, NY 10022
USA
Tel: (212) 826–9707
Fax: (212) 832–9493
Web: www.naadaa.org

Australian Antique Dealers'
Association
PO Box 24
Malvern
Victoria 3144
Australia
Tel: (03) 9576 2275
Fax: (03) 9576 2106
Web: www.aada.org.au
Email: secaada@ozemail.com.au

PICTURE CREDITS

INDEX

W.J. COOK & SONS

W.J. Cook & Sons was established by Bill Cook in 1962. His reputation for outstanding work quickly spread and since those early days clients have included the British Royal Household and Government, museums, leading collectors, dealers and private individuals. While still retaining a London workshop, the business is based in Marlborough, Wiltshire. With the cabinet-making, machine and polishing shops it is a business that is recognized as one of the leaders in its field. After training at the London College of Furniture, three of Bill's sons joined the business and have helped develop and further expand its range and facilities. Now their own children are being encouraged to pick up the tools with a view to taking the family tradition into a third generation.

The services carried out are many and include cabinet-making, gilding, carving, polishing, lock repairs, leathering and upholstery. Being a true family business it means that every restoration commission is undertaken with great care. With over 40 years of experience at the very highest level, together with an extensive in-house

Left: *from left to right, Bill, Stephen, Richard, Billy and (seated) Catherine Cook.*

library and access to furniture archives, any restoration carried out is authentic in every detail.

Virtually all the restoration work is still carried out using 18th- and 19th-century tools: their band saw was used in the construction of the panelling for the *Queen Mary*.

A final note: antique furniture if badly restored can rarely be returned to its original glory. Therefore, it is important that a suitably qualified restorer should be consulted when necessary.

High Trees House
Savernake Forest
Marlborough
Wiltshire
SN8 4NE
01672 513017
info@wjcookandsons.co.uk
www.wjcookandsons.co.uk

167 Battersea High Street
London
SW11 3JS
020 7736 5329

Author's acknowledgements

When approached to write this book we were delighted to accept. For a number of years we have been acutely aware of the absence of any book that was written and extensively photographed in a commercial restoration workshop and which showed and explained clearly how various techniques are carried out on a day to day basis. Drawing from over 40 years of experience and a lifetime's collection of materials and tools, we hope to have given the reader an authoritative insight into the subject.

While the overwhelming majority of work was undertaken "in house", there are grateful thanks due to others who have been invaluable in their help both with advice and in the use of their facilities: Barry Ansell of R.D. Robins Ltd,

London, on upholstery; Geoff Collier of Colliers Castings, Hooe, on casting methods; Les Crispin of Capital Crispin Veneer, London, on veneers, Alan Dallison on leathers, Bob Dunn of A. Dunn & Son, Chelmsford, on marquetry; and Optimum Brasses, Tiverton, on brassware.

Special thanks go to the staff in our workshops for making sure that the work needed for this book was always ready on time. A big thank you goes to Paul Lyon for his sterling work, without which this book would have been impossible.

On a personal note, like all family businesses, an unsung hero is our mother Catherine who has always been there keeping the wheels turning. Thanks also to my brothers Richard and Stephen with whom it is very much a team effort, and

not to forget Justin, who has chosen to follow his own path.

Thanks to all those who have been encouraging and supportive throughout the whole process of writing this book, including Richard my life-long friend, for his humour, often dispensed from across the world, Nathalie, whose words of wisdom, while not always fully appreciated are always carefully considered, and my three sons William, Henry and James, for just being themselves.

Finally this book is for my father from his sons, and for our sons and daughters from their fathers in the hope that they may one day take the business onwards for another generation.

BILLY COOK